I Promise To Stay Married (This Time)

Lea Hope Becker

ISBN: 1-4635-4576-2
ISBN-13: 9781463545765

Dedication

This book is dedicated to my beloved husband, Wayne Becker. Without his loving support, I would still be running around in circles, trying to find myself. He is the solid ground I have always needed in order to anchor my cloudlike fantasies.

TABLE OF CONTENTS

Acknowledgments

When I published my first book, I Promise To Keep Quiet (After I'm Dead), I bulldozed my way through it with very little input from others with the exception of my husband, Wayne Becker. His vision of the cover art for my first literary endeavor was a distinct improvement over mine. Also, he had been a professional illustrator, while I had been a dreamer and a doodler.

In preparing this story for publication I decided not to be such a lone wolf. I had coaching with my writing and editing assistance from a number of folks who also lent me moral support. Thanks to Iveth Thompson, who provided technical support; Laura Winger, who provided early favorable comment regarding my first book and encouraged me to write another; Ellen Weisberg, who was my inspiration for launching my writing for publication career and who has also provided advice as a publishing scout; and the members of my writing club, Pat Williams, Suzanne Lunsford, Bea Lewis, Charlie Sterbakov, Lee Roan and Lindy Freedman. I'd also like to acknowledge the mentorship of the leader of my intense writing workshop, Barbara Carter, whose guidance took me "from crayons to perfume" in the realm of editing and accuracy. Others to whom I am indebted are my friends: Barry Weiss, my constant source of support, suggesting some changes in my initial approach, Kiya Immergluck, who has assisted me for the last three years, and finally, my teacher at Broward College, Neil Plakcy, who directed me to the new world of E-book publishing. Finally, I'd like to thank my treasured publicist and editorial cheerleader, Sabrina Sumsion.

INTRODUCTION: THE IMPETUS BEHIND MY WRITING THIS BOOK

What made me want to get married again after two divorces? And why to him? What is it about this guy that keeps me hanging around? Being the analytical type, I needed to analyze my motives in order to justify my impetuosity. I entered into my third marriage with this man because he made my heart thump a lot. Lots of people marry for similar reasons and it doesn't always work out. I figured it was a good time for a review—you know, like the summary at the end of a chapter in a textbook, to see if you learned anything. Did I learn anything? Well, I wasn't finished with my studies. Maybe I'll never be finished, but I made a commitment, so I'm doing what I promised to do—stay married!

Then a light bulb flashed on. I looked at my husband of sixteen years and suddenly the truth came to me—I really loved the man I married—you could call it a first for me. But how did I know that IT was the real thing after so many years of trying to find IT?

It's simple: He wasn't the man in my fairy tale! Yet I have stuck with him and cannot envision ever wanting IT otherwise. Does that mean that my fairy tale was misleading? You be the judge. Read my story.

Here's the way my husband appears to me: (1) he is disciplined and principled to the point of robotic precision; (2) he has lost most of his hair and doesn't seem to want it back, while I worry myself to death if I see a strand of mine in the sink; (3) he is sarcastic as hell, but almost always only to me; (4) he considers me self-absorbed, while I think <u>he</u> is the self-absorbed party, but then I'm probably too self-absorbed to see the whole picture; and (5) he thinks that when women cry they are just plain nuts, and I'm big at crying. To make matters even more challenging for a fixer-upper wife like me, he weighs himself once a day and checks his net worth once a month. That's sooooo, like, confident! I check my net worth once a day and weigh myself when I'm able to deal with the fear.

Some things in life are simply easier for him than they are for me, but many things are otherwise. I might add that during our marriage I have been happier than I could ever have imagined.

He helped me realize my creative nature by not accidentally throwing out my edited manuscripts when he emptied the trash baskets, even when my efforts littered the floor. He also demonstrated his dedication to my work by drawing the cover of this book after I hurled numerous threats at him. Actually, they were only mild threats. I've learned to tone down my demands. At the same time he began to accept that I was serious about writing for publication and that I would be prudent as to how I was going to handle my promotion and budget while I pursued my new career goal.

God bless husbands who care enough to stay with their wives for as long as it takes.

Chapter 1
FRIENDS AND LETTERS

The phone on the Lucite end table next to me rang just as the sex-starved couple had begun to tear off their clothes. I picked up the receiver and hesitated for just an instant while I lowered the volume on the remote. "Hello?"

It was my best and most loyal friend, Annie. I could feel the rhythm of my breathing speed up as I prepared to deliver the telephone speech which had been playing in my head all day. Should I just tell her my news, or should I also tell her that our mutual friend, Sarah, had stung me to the core that morning? Maybe I should just let the conversation happen in a genteel manner. "No," I second-guessed myself, "I'll just spew out what I'm thinking no matter what I planned to say—it's too late for me to learn to measure my words."

I turned off the TV altogether. From the receiver there came a burst of girlish exuberance. "I can't believe it! I just can't believe it!" Annie could believe it, but women friends everywhere know that certain common expressions mean the opposite.

"Oh, Hi there," I said in as neutral a tone as I could muster, wiping a few specks of dirty film off the mouthpiece with a tissue from my pocket, "I think I know what you're about to say." I was already kicking myself for not giving Annie the inside story first. She deserved better.

"Well, if you know what I'm about to say, then why don't you tell me what I think you're dying to tell me?"

"I'm going to tell you what you're dying to know. I was just going to call you," I lied. Actually, I was going to call her later—maybe a day later.

"OK, I'm waiting. Let's hear it!"

"Uh, yes, here's the unvarnished truth—I'm getting married again."

"I had to hear you utter those words, even though I was picking up waves."

"So, Annie, how did you find out? Telepathy or Sarah?" Lately, Sarah's gossipy ways had exhausted my patience.

"Sarah called me this morning. She was out of her mind and probably off her medication!" Annie seemed more emotionally stirred up than I had sensed in a long time. She had a big booming musical voice. I loved her enthusiastic approach to everything—whether she sounded muted or turned on like a theatre marquee. She even cried her heart out with more gusto than most folks did when the situation warranted.

The volume of Annie's voice returned to normal as she carried on. "You're leaving your home, your kids, your law practice, everything? Is that right?

"That's about it, Annie. I'm really leaving Illinois for good. I'll be moving to my new husband's home—it's located in a very small town in Ulster County, New York."

"Wow! I knew you were hot for this guy you knew from high school—what was it, forty some years ago? When we met him at the restaurant last week I did sense some chemistry there—but do you remember what you said to me in the ladies' room?"

"Uh, yaah, I told you I was just being polite to him or something like that."

"My God, girl, this switch in you is rather sudden, isn't it? I mean, well, it's just great, but didn't you just recently swear, I mean swear emphatically, that you were NEVER GETTING SERIOUS AGAIN! "

In that instant that transpires when you are being held accountable for your declarations, I groped for a decent response. "I guess I did. I've had a major change of heart!" I winced at my friend's razor-sharp memory. She had a way of remembering the details of my slimiest dating experiences.

"I guess I should fill you in a bit," I added, as I glanced at my framed print of a dancing Mickey Mouse, hung purposely on my white wall right next to Annie's framed abstract painting of inner space. It was confession time. "You see, he bowled me over. I mean, I roped him. Well, uh, we roped each other." I heard a pause on the other end, so I kept talking. "And just what did Sarah say behind my back?"

"You know Sarah and how jaded she can be. She told me you were making the biggest mistake of your life."

"Well, I think she feels that way for a lot of reasons I can almost understand. Still, she could have wished me well. What do you think?"

"I think you're in love."

"Come on, what else?"

"You're right about Sarah. She's either jealous or thinks she's a psychic or both. Well, don't worry about her. She can't stand my boyfriend, Art, either."

"I do worry about her and her situation, being so alone and anti-men like she is. She had me in tears when I needed a boost. Listen, I'll have to call you back. The dude is going to phone any minute and I told him I'd be home. I'll give you all the lurid details later!"

"OK, but why do you call him a dude?"

"You saw what he was wearing when we were at the restaurant?"

"Uh, all I noticed was his hand creeping along your knee."

"Come on!"

"Well, he was wearing a green polo shirt with a pencil poking out of a pocket and had removed his baseball hat. He's one of the cutest going bald fellows I've ever seen. Sexy, quite sexy. Plus, he was a Yankee fan."

"Yes, he was positively green—I mean green, as in unsophisticated. He dresses like a hick and he likes dressing like a hick. You'll never see any flowers on <u>his</u> shirts, kid. He hates sissy clothes." I stopped there, being careful not to blurt out that he had disliked the inner space painting she had sold to me because he thought it looked like a picture of an embryo inside a balloon. I had bought it because I thought the painting was an abstract of my life.

"You looked so pretty that night," Annie continued. "I like the highlights in your hair—the red is so much more you than that blonde color—"

"Another vote for the red!" I exclaimed.

"I also loved—really loved—that multi-colored sweater over your black slacks. I think it was slenderizing. You two actually look like you fit well together."

"I did lose a few pounds," I mused, choosing to ignore her two-of-a-kind inference, as I could feel my pulse speed up and simultaneously detect a shimmy in my right hand. Annie had uttered the word "slenderizing."

Early that morning I had given myself a session with the bathroom scale. There was a ritual which I followed: After removing my towel and standing naked and shivering right out of the whirlpool tub, I would gingerly put my full weight on the scale. My tendency was to hang onto the towel bar for moral support, but I usually shrugged off the dishonesty and then bravely let my hand drop to my side. Today the needle stopped at 135, which meant that my monk-like lunches of eight ounces of vegetable soup had paid off. My cheeks were not quite as plump as they had been only a few weeks ago!

I had been squirming around on my loveseat in the protective confines of my upstairs loft. "Annie, will you excuse me? Can I call you tomorrow?" I heard myself pleading.

"Yes, you don't feel like talking any longer, right?"

"Bingo! You're the psychic, really, and I'm still reeling from my conversation with Sarah."

"I'm aware she can be hurtful" Annie continued, "but she does have a gift for sniffing out secrets, don't you think?"

"She sniffs too much—I need friends, not a hound dog."

"I'll let you go, but we girls were all asking each other, and we couldn't figure it out—what the hell does this dude do for a living?"

"Oh, he's retired, uh huh, retired."

"Retired from what, please?"

"You're not going to believe it when I tell you."

"A farmer?"

"No. He bought a chicken farm, but he never tried to make a living off that."

"So what then?"

"If you're standing, you'd better sit, Annie, because I know how hard you work to scrape a living from selling your paintings."

"Don't tell me——"

"Yes, he's a retired artist." The breathing on the other end stopped. "Annie? ANNIE??"

"I'm here," she replied quietly. "Oh, everything's OK, but let's talk later. I have to see a collector about a bad check."

As I said goodbye and hung up, I wondered if I should have explained to Annie that my fiancé was actually a retired commercial artist, although he called himself a humorous illustrator. I could also have mentioned to her that he was some strange variety of miser—in other words, my direct opposite—but that information would have required a longer conversation.

I walked barefoot over to my small desk in the spare bedroom, feeling the peach plush carpet on the balls and toes of my feet. The upper left-hand corner of that little designer gem from Pier One held a pile of credit card bills which needed attention. The right-hand corner held my emotional pot of gold. Atop a square of aluminum foil was a significantly high stack of letters which I had been accumulating. I had stuck one of those Post-It® notes to the top of the pile. It read: "love letters—avoid contact with wood or other flammable surface."

By now the cuckoo clock over the desk was chirping 9PM. I wasn't really expecting a call from my intended because I knew it was his gun club meeting night. Scrutinizing which bills I should pay didn't seem like much fun, so I turned my attention to the letters. I began to reread, for the fourth or fifth time, each of the earliest of them. That helped. I refolded and returned each precious writing to its envelope, being careful to put the right one with the right postmark. Only a few tears trickled now as I stared at the calligraphic style of the hot-blooded gent's handwriting. Something compelled me to once again read the very first one he had sent—a mere two months earlier. It had been typed on wide-ruled loose-leaf notebook paper. My eyes jumped to the paragraph that had brought my surging blood vessels to a throbbing intensity. Its first sentence began: "When I got your letter, it was such a nice surprise. It was just as though all the years had not changed you. You sound like the same sweet girl I admired before you knew I existed. Maybe you've had some sad stuff in your life, but so have I. My wife died and you've been divorced twice. So now you're a lawyer. It's not a big shock because I always knew you were ambitious...."

The rest of his letter described his life living in the Upstate New York area in a turn-of-the-century country cottage. His words were friendly and warm, like a pair of comfortable old shoes, but my reaction was intensely emotional—a therapist's meat and potatoes. The first time I read them my composure went into a tailspin. "What is it about these simple friendly words that has me going into a near panic attack?" I shrieked to myself, as I tried to remember the Way We Were. My carefully guarded floodgates opened up as the possibilities of a romance seemed possible. I had cried off and on uncontrollably for the remainder of that day and added two boxes of Kleenex® to my shopping list.

"Thank God I'm more composed now," I assured myself, as I replaced those five pages in the proper envelope and returned it to the stack. It was next to the bottom. Only my retained copy of my very first letter to him—the cheerful message which had served as an invitation—was below it. I thought about calling Annie back that evening to pour my heart out, but dropped the idea. I didn't have the energy.

One hour later, I was clad in the nightgown I had purchased two days before his first visit. After leaving that satiny creation unlaundered for weeks because the smell of his after-shave was still on it, I had finally thrown it in the washer with my other delicates, making a note to ask him what kind of men's cologne he liked. Before I fell asleep, I remembered something else—he had whispered to me that I was his very favorite scent. Yiiiikes! At least <u>he</u> was honest. Who was the hypocrite here? Me, the middle-aged Cosmo-leaning woman who acted like Mother Theresa, or him—the saint who had been completely faithful to his wife?

I rolled my body around and around in the bed we had made love in and felt the peach-colored down comforter against my lustful 135-pound body. I hadn't dared to put that comforter in the laundry, and vowed that I never would.

Chapter 2
PLOTTING THE
ESCAPE

I woke up to the sound of garbage being gobbled up by one of those stinking refuse trucks that nobody can live without. The snooze alarm went off, but I ignored it, as usual. My nightgown had a chokehold on my neck, so I figured I had been having one of those salty dreams again. Oh yeah, wasn't there a paw on my rear end that wasn't mine? With stardust still beclouding my mind, I heard the phone on my dressing table ring. I tried to raise myself to a sitting position, but not every muscle cooperated. The third ring of the telephone now jolted me into a fuller measure of wakefulness, as I realized that I was alone except for the Gund® teddy bear resting on my pillow. I stared at that spongy cuddly object which never needed to be fed and kept my bedroom behavior secret.

"Should I let that answering machine do its thing?" I asked myself, as I ducked under the covers for a third cycle of the snooze alarm. "Oh no!" I shrieked suddenly, bounding out of bed and rushing over to the phone like a kid with a new toy. I had almost forgotten why I set the alarm clock so carefully. "Hello and good morning," I sputtered, rubbing my eyes and groping for my eyeglasses.

"You sound breathless—did I wake you up?" The husky voice on the other end was the Loverman's now familiar baritone. Even when he wasn't chanting the words to one of his bluegrass favorites or Irish ditties, I could hear the music.

In my haste to answer the call, I had stubbed my middle toe on the table leg and hoped it wasn't about to swell up. Although I still wasn't fully awake, I felt a warm glow and a sense of relief that the caller wasn't my younger son—the one who never slept. That kid would have hounded me about some money problem of his which had no solution or some new illness he had contracted which had no antidote.

"No, you didn't wake me up, honey, the garbage truck was squealing and then the phone rang. How are you and what time is it?"

"In my town it's 9AM—in yours it's only eight. I'm off to the Albany airport in an hour and called to remind you to pick me up at O'Hare at about three o'clock."

"You didn't have to remind me, but I love that you called anyway. I'm still wearing my nightgown—the peach one with the spaghetti straps that fall off my shoulders."

"Not now, dumpling, I still have some last-minute packing to do, and I have no time to fantasize. Did anyone make reservations for dinner with those friends of yours?"

"Yes. We'll be dining with Annie the artist, Sarah the psychic and Glenda the zombielike nurse. Glenda's six foot four, but she's really down to earth."

"Is that supposed to be a pun? Say, about this restaurant you're dragging me to—I'm being interviewed, aren't I?"

"No, sweetie, I'm just fulfilling my script—I have to break my tether with these females very carefully—they have no idea that we're engaged! I told them you were coming to town to see me about business matters and that you were a good friend."

"Even ditsy airhead females won't believe that bullshit."

"I told them we weren't serious at all."

"What are you worried about?"

"It's just Sarah—she's been trying to convert me to her religion and when she finds out I'm leaving town, she won't take it very well. Listen, I have to do this my way! Please play along!"

"I'll do it just this once, but your kids know, so how can you keep it from your girlfriends?"

"I can't much longer, but for tonight, it's easy. The kids don't even know you're coming to town."

"I'd better get going. I'll see you at the American Airlines baggage claim. I can't wait. Oh, where are we going for dinner?"

"To one of the Greektown places. You like Greek food, don't you?"

"I love Greek food, but you told me that you didn't, so why there?"

"Oh, Sarah's Greek and she picked it out. I let her have her way because if she starts arguing with those lungs of hers, the statues in Athens could crumble!"

"Goodbye, dear, see you in about seven hours!"

I hung up dazed and excited that the five foot seven hero on the other end of the phone line was practically mine. Too bad I hated Greek food. I liked Greek style, however, even some Greek men. I slowly made my way to my spacious walk-in closet, attempting to recall the name of the only Greek guy I had ever gotten excited about. Oh yeah, it had been at least ten years ago. I even remembered my anticipation before going on that date and the conversation I had engaged in with Annie at the time. While rummaging in my closet looking for my brand new Carole Little® ensemble and the matching Ferragamo® pumps, that first phone conversation about the Greek came back to me as though it was only a week ago. Of course, I usually began our conversations like a reckless schoolgirl:

✳✳✳

"Annie, it's me—got a minute?" She had to know I was lying about that "one minute" promise because I never kept it.

"Go ahead—I know you're calling about a potential conquest—I can paint while I talk."

"You know that famous Greek restaurant on Broadway?"

"Oh, the Terrace?"

"Yeah, well the owner's son asked me out and I'm going."

"That family is very wealthy, I heard. But I don't see you being with a person like that."

"I think he's cute and you're right, he absolutely reeks of money. But hell, it's just a date."

"Watch out for Greeks bearing gifts imbedded in sperm!"

"That's terrible!"

"Is he tall?"

"Oh, only six foot, I think. I can handle a six-footer."

"Not a rich Greek one."

"If it doesn't work out, I promise I'll never even dream of getting serious again! That is, unless he treats me like a princess!"

"Good luck, kid. My last date with that fellow, Harold, you know, the real estate lawyer I went with two years ago, well, no matter how hard I tried, I couldn't get him to commit."

"I remember—every time you turned on the charm your efforts just died."

"Well, that's an interesting choice of words. Guess what? He died! I just found out."

"You're giving me the bull! How old was he?"

"Fifty-one."

"What happened?"

"He was going with Leeanne at the time. She wouldn't talk about it, but I found out he keeled over at a house closing. Can you beat that?"

"That's such a shame—you really liked him, at least for awhile."

"The thrill had worn off to tell the truth, but I feel bad for Leeanne."

"I wonder if the house got sold that day."

"You're too much. Have fun on your hot date!"

"Gee, I wonder if this guy, Jimmy's healthy! He drinks a lot of that Ouzo, I know, but he says he holds it well. Shit, what if I have to drink that stuff? Oh, I guess I can fake it."

✸✸✸

Spotting the outfit I was looking for, all carefully suspended by the hanger straps, I grabbed it and hung it on the doorknob of the entry to my private bath and prepared to make the bed. My bed making routine was so automatic I could plan my day and solve a legal problem while smoothing down the comforter and propping up the pillow shams. But my memory of the brief encounter with that Greek guy continued to fill my head. I remembered swearing to myself that I would never again let a man like that think he could take advantage of me on a first date, no matter how delicious he looked. That character had treated me like a body without a brain and had tried to get me drunk. "Now why am I dwelling on a gruesome dating experience now, when my true love is landing here in a few hours?" I scolded myself sometimes because who else would?

The phone rang again and I answered it quickly. It was my daughter.

"Mom?"

"What are you doing up so early, honey?" I thought something was wrong because she never called before 11AM. I had raised a child the opposite of me—a total night owl.

"Oh, are you busy tonight? I thought Nancy and I might take a drive over and keep you company!"

"I'm sorry, sweetie. I'm meeting Sarah and Annie—uh, we planned it a week ago!"

"Well, it was just a thought!"

"Listen, honey, I have to cram for a client and can't talk now. I'll call you back!"

"OK, do it tomorrow, huh?" I'm working this afternoon."

"Sure, that's fine. Bye, dear!" I hung up the phone, feeling guilty for the fib. My daughter didn't know yet that my fiancé was coming in. I hated myself when I did that, but I had to go through with my half thought through plan. I bathed, dressed and put on my makeup like I was getting ready for a screen test. The plan for this day was promising to be the challenge of the week, or maybe the month—keeping my engagement secret until I could integrate the reality of it into my psyche.

***

At Chicago's O'Hare Airport, it's not unusual for people to run up to one another by the baggage carousel and kiss each other exuberantly, but most of the time it happens before the luggage arrives. Well, this time it was different. My fiancé saw me and waved and gestured for me to be seated on a nearby bench. I was puzzled because the picture in my head was that I would run over to him and throw my arms around his neck. Something was amiss, but he was holding a suitcase, so I ran up to him anyway. I noticed that there was a white fabric band apparently holding the suitcase together.

"What happened?"

"I'm sorry, honey, I'm happy as hell to see you, but as the bag came off the carousel, the thing opened and spilled my clothes out on the floor. I think those baggage handlers broke my lock!"

16

"That white thing holding your suitcase together looks like a belt from a terrycloth robe."

"It is a belt from my robe! It's all I had handy!"

I suddenly felt nervous about something, but shrugged it off. "Oh, well, we can buy you a new suitcase, darling, can't we?"

"What? Replace this perfectly wonderful genuine leather multiple-compartmented traveling gem? I'll repair it myself, but for now, let's just get the car and drive to your place where I can change clothes. Also, I'm starved."

I looked at the gerry-rigged battered old suitcase swinging from his hand while he walked ahead of me hurriedly, forcing me to run to keep up. I had to shout to be heard by him in the crowded terminal, but it was necessary because he was headed in the wrong direction.

"Where are you going? The exit to the parking is the other way!"

"Isn't this the way to the men's room?"

"Uh, of course, I wasn't thinking, honey. It's over there next to the water fountain."

"Watch my bag, OK?"

"I'll guard it carefully," I promised. He lowered the suitcase to the floor and it fell over on its side. Then came the passionate kiss and embrace which I had hoped would have occurred in a different area, but I forced myself not to be disconcerted by the stares of guys making a beeline for the rest room.

Chapter 3
THE RESTAURANT

Getting around anywhere near Chicago's Loop on a Saturday evening was always a crapshoot. Even with my good nose for avoiding traffic snarls, we arrived at the restaurant a half hour late. There was a jam-up on the Edens and the worst of the bottleneck was where the expressway was all lit up, so we couldn't do much fooling around in the car. Actually, I was the one who was scared silly that some other driver would see me steering while my passenger was groping most of me. He finally sat up straight as we entered Hubbard's Cave—that tunnel on the fringe of the Loop where driving nightmares occurred regularly. The ramp was clear and as we exited at the Adams Street turnoff, he froze in his seat as my tires squealed while I was making the sharp turn. "Sorry about that." I felt compelled to apologize for my aggressive moves behind the wheel, adding, "I'm great at getting places, but sloppy at turns."

"It's OK, I've had white knuckles before. I love you, but maybe next time I'll drive."

"That's good, because you're going to need to remember that feeling you have for me when Sarah starts up with her psychobabble."

"I'll keep my mouth shut about her psychedelic bullshit and turn the conversation to knitting and PTA meetings."

"Dear, I know you're being sarcastic, but don't forget that none of these girls has kids!"

"Oh, I did forget. Well, are they virgins?"

18

"Annie has been in several relationships, Glenda is still legally married to her wife-beater estranged husband, and Sarah was abused, allegedly sexually, by her two brothers when she was twelve, and hasn't dated anybody that I'm aware of for about twenty-five years. Also, she's a rather large woman."

"Oh, then I'll skip the knitting and PTA references. I'll talk about my pistol prowess and hunting trips—how's that?"

"Sarah and Glenda are knee-jerk leftists, although Annie is open-minded. Better stick to the safe subjects: high school proms, the weather, and how wonderful the Greek menu is at this paragon of Chicago cuisine."

"What if the food isn't good?"

"That's the last thing I'm worried about."

The hostess greeted us with a smile and an evaluation. "Your party of five is under the name Angelou?" She checked her guest list and signaled a very tall thin man, who would be escorting us to our table. He needed to be thin because he had to thread his way between several very narrow spaces between the tables. While we were trying to follow the fellow to the next room, I looked around the trendy establishment with its indirect lighting exposing myriads of paintings of famous Grecian landmarks. Customers were having one hell of a raucous time of it and several were singing and holding their glasses like they were toasting the Next Coming. I always glanced at diners' plates to see what seemed appetizing, but all I could see here that appealed to me was some half-eaten pastitsio. The calorie count for two bites of it would be a diet buster. One lady waiter barely avoided us as she glided over to a table balancing a huge tray of sizzling food. Another waiter ran around filling peoples' water glasses and I wondered why everyone looked so happy in such a madhouse. Strolling musicians made the rounds adding to the din.

My fiancé spoke into my ear: "I carry earplugs for a situation like this, but I suppose that would seem anti-social, wouldn't it?"

"Are you just kidding, or what?"

"It was just a thought, honey. I guess I'll have to get through this interview without them!"

"It's not an interview! I've already hired you!"

"I think you've got it backwards—I'm the one with the wallet."

"Oh, I can chip in, if you'd like."

"Next time."

Finally, the slender fellow guided us over to a table in a corner situated under a painting of the Parthenon where my three friends were already seated. There was a slight chance that we might be able to hear ourselves talking to each other. The ladies each stood up to shake hands with the man I had described as a nice person who had been painfully shy in his youth. Annie was two inches taller than him, Sarah was four inches taller and Glenda had to stoop to meet his gaze. It occurred to me that I was taking a chance displaying my sweetheart to my rabid feminist friends, but he seemed to take it in stride. After asking each of them for their names, his voice boomed out above the din of the music:

"The drinks and all the food are on me, girls, so don't argue! I'm an old-fashioned male chauvinist who won't let a lady pay!"

Nobody argued and even if one of them had a thought to do so, it wouldn't have made any difference. The musicians came over to our table and serenaded us while the Ouzo flowed and the chatter and laughter of the other guests rose to a fever pitch. This scene was not what I had planned. I reached for a slice of what I thought was garlic bread, but it seemed rather brittle, and I gave up trying to reach the butter. Everyone was talking at once and firing questions at me which I couldn't hear, so I kept shouting: "What? How's that again? You like my outfit? Oh, you're asking if I want my candle lit?" I gave up trying to converse.

Frustration set in for me, even though everyone seemed to be enjoying themselves. Annie was the lead conversationalist and asked lots of friendly questions, which my fiancé answered enthusiastically. One of the questions was whether he missed Chicago. I had to hide my smirk because I knew he was ecstatic that he didn't have to live there any longer. There was a ready-made smile on his face which looked to me like it had been plastered there without being connected to his neural network. Sure enough, he was kicking my leg a little under the table. If I hadn't been so tense, I would have burst out laughing.

"I'll tell you what I love best about Chicago," he nearly shouted.

"Oh no," I thought, cringing, what's he going to say now?

"I just love the waterfront. My family used to take me to Foster Beach when I was a kid and that's where I got my first sex education."

Glenda laughed, Annie shrieked in delight and Sarah curled her mouth into the opposite of a happy face. This man I had fallen for had more surprises up his sleeve than most magicians, but I knew that some people did not appreciate being teased, and he could be merciless. As for me, I just put forth my cute face and wished I had worn something without long sleeves when I got olive oil on one of the cuffs. I tried to hide all the crumbs I had left on the table in a futile attempt to break the slice of bread cleanly. Not one of my three friends seemed to notice or care that I barely sipped from my glass.

At one point I looked to see if my fiancé was enjoying his food and noticed a hint of a glassy-eyed look about him. Had he reached his quota of girl talk? Maybe it was indigestion. Maybe it was time to consider winding things up.

I don't remember much more about the conversation that evening, but I suspected that Sarah had figured out that my so-called casual friend was more than just a date, when she called him my boyfriend in more than audible tones. When she wasn't gulping wine or wolfing down huge portions of roast lamb and stuffed grape leaves, she scowled most of the time until the dessert arrived. Helping herself to two generous servings of chocolate-covered baklava, she smiled pleasantly just prior to passing out and knocking over her wine glass. I looked around the place for a waiter or somebody to assist, but Glenda, like the good nurse she was, anticipated her pal's drunken stupor and slapped her around a bit until the woman came to.

"Sarah shouldn't be eating chocolate," she offered, "she's diabetic and allergic and can't tolerate alcohol very well."

"Then why did she drink so much?" I queried naively.

Glenda gave me a look that told me to avoid the subject. After we had finished our dinner and the bill was paid, she whispered to me:

"Your date picked up the tab, and that was very nice of him, but Sarah would have been better off if she had to use her own money. You know, I'm sure, that she's poverty-stricken."

I should have known, but I didn't realize until then that the only thing that kept her sober was her meager budget. The woman should have been a missionary in a foreign country, but not everybody has the career they are best suited for. I expected to get an earful from Sarah the next day and it would not be pleasant. I needed a friend like her like I needed a migraine headache. As we were making our exit, each of us being careful not to knock anything off any of the tables because of the tight aisle space, I began to relax a bit. Our dining experience ended about the same time as the strains of "Never On Sunday" began.

Chapter 4
PRACTICING TOGETHERNESS

My fiancé and I left the restaurant and searched for my car in the parking lot. I became a tad panicky when we didn't find it right away until I remembered that we had been unable to get into the parking lot when we arrived and that we had parked on the street. I was holding onto him for dear life because he seemed a bit wobbly. "Are you OK?" I expected him to nod that he was, but that wasn't his response.

"I probably shouldn't have drunk so much on an empty stomach," he said. "You just get us to your place and I'll be all right."

I found the car just where I left it and excused him for not opening up the driver's side door for me. Actually, I opened the passenger's side door for him and made sure he was able to fasten the seat belt. I drove at a sensible pace and struggled to think of a clever way to comment on the evening we had just survived. It wasn't necessary because he began to snore softly within a few minutes. There is something momentous about hearing one's heartthrob's first animal noises in a new relationship. It's neither romantic nor disgusting—it's just real life. I got us safely to my townhouse forty miles north of Greektown and wondered if I should make some coffee. As we pulled into my driveway he woke up.

"Are we here?"

"Yes, honey, are _you_ here?"

"I'm fine. The queasiness is gone, I guess. You're a good driver and I'm sorry I needled you earlier."

I guessed that he complimented me on my driving because nothing seemed to interrupt his snooze in the car. As we walked into the house he appeared so normal I figured we would dive right into bed. Again I misjudged him. When he had changed clothes and cleaned up earlier that day, he had left his suitcase downstairs in the foyer. Now I noticed that he was pausing for a few moments to stare at it. He checked his watch and then turned to me.

"Are you sleepy? He surprised me again. Of course I was sleepy, but not <u>that</u> sleepy.

"Oh, not very. What's on your mind?"

"Well, honey, I left my suitcase downstairs in plain sight to remind myself about the broken lock. I think I should fix it before I lose my ambition!" He prodded me up the stairs toting the thing behind him and we entered my bedroom. "Your little bear is waiting for you," he joked. I enjoyed how he noticed things when I didn't realize it. He had commented about how nicely I had furnished that room the first time he saw it, but not until we had first surrendered to each other in a burst of pent-up desire.

✳✳✳

Engaging in conversation in order to alleviate nervousness was a habit I employed. The tension of discovering an old feeling which had been sealed off for so many years was overwhelming. I simply had to discuss everything, and now I had a captive partner.

"Do you remember much about what was going on with us forty years ago?" I asked him a few minutes after our first intimate encounter.

"I remember that we nearly made love one evening, but I was afraid."

"Of consequences?"

"Yes, the consequences were pretty severe in those days. Things have changed a lot."

"It's not just that we're so much older now and that our inhibitions have melted—it's something else."

"Like your experience with unhappy marriages?"

"Yes, that and just learning about what my real needs are."

"Your needs are met now, aren't they?"

"Well, I don't want just today—I want tomorrow also!"

"I'm thinking, you want a real teddy bear!"

My thoughts were happy ones. I looked him straight in the eye and said: "You always used to come up with a meaningful joke when I started to feel blue—when I was a teen-ager back then—but you've probably forgotten all about that. Except you're doing it now again, and I love you for it!"

"And I love you for lots of things, but stop talking so much!"

I didn't realize until that moment that all my life I had been wasting a lot of words which were probably not required. "Oh, of course," I responded, feeling somewhat chided. I mentally clamped my mouth shut and waited for him to say something romantic. When that didn't occur, I felt compelled to fill in the awkward pause.

"Uh, are you going to keep ribbing me about that teddy bear?"

"No. I want you to change companions!"

"Oh, well, the poor little thing was available when I didn't have <u>you</u> to keep me company!" We both began to laugh.

✳✳✳

"Let me get this damned suitcase lock fixed and then we can both be relaxed." He set it down and removed all the clothing and other contents, placing them on the rug. He put his pajamas on the bed and dug out a travel bag and brought it into the bathroom. Then he rummaged through his stuff and got out his handy little repair kit and fixed the lock in less than ten minutes. I watched him manipulate the small tools with amazement, because my previous two husbands had been all thumbs. Certainly, neither of them would have traveled with a tool kit.

I urgently needed some gesture of affection. He stood up and looked at me with a great big smile and then came the great big hug—it was a long one. Neither of us spoke. I did not find his embraces relaxing—I found them simultaneously stimulating and nerve-wracking, like a young lady who has just been asked to dance by a new partner and doesn't quite know the steps.

He loosened his grip and asked, "Honey, do you want me to shave again? Feel my cheeks." I put my hand on his face where there once was a young boy's fuzz and two deep dimples. His eyes had the same greenish hazel iris coloring that I had long ago once written about in a love poem. When he smiled I noticed that the dimples had turned to creases and his neck showed wrinkles that he didn't seem to worry about. I usually tried to cover up mine with a scarf. I had gotten accustomed to the fact that my vision of my teenaged boyfriend with the fifties pompadour had to be altered a bit. The man I had promised to marry now sported a serious moustache and a fairly thick beard which had begun to turn grey.

"Oh, you mean you sometimes shave more than once a day? Well, yes, if you want to. Can I watch?"

"Sure—come into the bathroom and keep me company."

I followed him and stared as he unzipped the black travel case and removed a bar of unscented soap, a red-handled shaving brush that looked like it dated from the Great Depression and a straight razor that resembled one that my father had.

"Where did you get that razor?"

"It belonged to my dad. I have three like this. Nobody sells them any more." I didn't doubt it. I was engaged to a man two months younger than me who liked old things. Was that why he had fallen for me—a girl from his past? Did I really care? An even more important point occurred to me that evening as he fell asleep after a brief attempt at passion under the warmth of my peach comforter: Would he really treat me like a princess? Then I remembered a conversation we had had several weeks earlier about the subject of an engagement ring.

✱✱✱

I was the one who brought up the sensitive issue with some fear that I might sound like a gold-digging type where money and appearances were important to me. They were. So I tried some tact:

"My first husband and I went to the jewelry store together to pick out rings."

"Oh, were you thinking about having me give you an engagement ring?"

"Well, not exactly."

"What then?"

"I think I take after my mother."

"That's not an answer."

"I don't want to sound greedy."

"My best friend's wife has lots of jewelry. You met Arnie and Peg when you visited, remember? Well, Peg buys stuff for herself and has to sneak it into the house because Arnie thinks she has enough baubles to last for three generations."

This conversation wasn't going the way I had hoped. Was it incumbent on me to take up the challenge and morph into someone who could be happy living on the cheap? Aah, frugality, it never ran in my family.

"I opt for no engagement ring because, uh, because, well, you don't have to."

"Good."

✱✱✱

The man I was promised to lay flat on his back sound asleep. I lay on my side watching the lump under the comforter move up and down with his breathing. The only light in the room came from the rays of the street lamp below through the window. Soon I would be leaving this bedroom for good. I managed to relax and relinquish my gaze, but even as I got into sleeping position my thoughts rambled on in a continuing reverie. It ended that evening with the following silent prayer on my part:

"Please dear God, let this man lying next to me in this designer platform bed be the man I need him to be—bestowing upon my soul all the love and attention I crave. Also, God, could you give me the wisdom to figure out how to get my wardrobe and my art collection into that tiny house in the sticks in the middle of nowhere?"

✳✳✳

I didn't quite get God's answer, but that conversation regarding an engagement ring proved to be more than merely unnerving. It had me groping for some sort of redeeming move—one that would propel me into a new realm of pragmatism. As soon as my fiancé left town, I made arrangements to attend the O'Hare Antique and Jewelry Show, which was beginning the following weekend in Chicago. I went there like a trouper and sold $1,000 worth of jewelry, reasoning that I had to take action before I chickened out.

That evening I called Annie again to give her the latest scoop. "Am I interrupting anything?" I asked in such a way that she would feel duty-bound to say no.

"No," she answered, "I was just wrapping up this waterfall piece I did—you know, that commission I told you about."

"Annie, I've had a remarkable switcheroo! I'm being transformed!"

"Oh, did you tell Sarah off or something?"

"No, I sold a thousand bucks worth of necklaces and bracelets!"

"That's so interesting. Why?"

"Well, you know I've always knocked myself for acting like a Jewish Princess!"

"Being something like a Jewish Princess is a major part of your persona, dear. But you've worked very hard in your life to reinvent yourself as a caring soul and a skilled professional. You shouldn't knock yourself down for anything!"

"Well now I'm a Jewish Princess without much jewelry!"

"That's OK, isn't it?"

"It's not only OK—it's perfect. I didn't need it! All that I needed was my Prince!"

Chapter 5
DON'T CRY FOR ME, ILLINOIS

My fiancé rested against the driver's side fender of his rental car and looked at me as though I were an angel he had summoned. I had discovered that hugging a man who offered dreams for a fabulous future covered up the trembling, so I wrapped my arms around him tightly.

He grinned at my exuberance. "Hey, we'll see each other in three weeks at my place!" That's all he had to say to keep me breathing without interruption. We had arrived at the moment of parting. I could not separate hope from reality at that moment, but I relished the hope as a gift from God. The guy who had traveled from Upstate New York just to reunite with me was not a devil tempting me to throw my old life away—he was simply a man who suggested that if I were willing to make serious changes he would be there to ease the pain.

As I bid him goodbye and watched the car disappear at the end of the cul-de-sac, I tried to recall the key conversation word for word that had taken place only two months earlier. We were standing on my patio a face apart....

✻✻✻

Summoning all the courage I had stored up for the moment of truth which was about to arrive, I let the words come tumbling forth: "I'm not interested in occasional dates across state lines," I said, peering into those soulful wells of expression—praying that I had read his intentions accurately. I desperately needed the same hungry look of approval that first stirred me at age fifteen.

"What is it that would work for you?" he asked in a muted voice. He seemed caught in the throes of indecision—that sticky place where a fellow's pulsating hormones collide with his fear of lifelong loss of freedom. It's a place that women who have been around the block recognize long before the unsuspecting male realizes he's in the process of being hooked.

"I wouldn't be happy with any long distance arrangement," I answered, staring at the twitching in his face. He seemed to be getting the picture.

"I'll have to give this some deep thought," he stammered.

"I understand." Then a few protracted minutes passed, punctuated by some shallow breathing. Had he decided to put his cards on the table? I knew that my hand had been dealt face up for the entire world to see, while I waited for his response.

"Well, do you love me as much as I love you?"

"I do love you, but I think I know what's in the way, don't you?

"Yes, it's the distance. You know I don't want to live in Illinois."

"I know. I could easily leave Illinois."

"Would you really pull up stakes and come with me, like be my country wife?" There—he had uttered the word "wife." The proposal to propose had been delivered. Was that a cheering section for me I imagined I was hearing? Had my hook landed the big fish?

I began to resume regular breathing as the hard part was over. Now I didn't need a prepared script to follow. He seemed to respond to cuteness bordering on silly, where I could relax and let my mouth do its spontaneous thing. "Let's see—do you really own twenty acres with hundreds of big trees on them?"

"Twenty-one and a half."

"That just about settles it then. I suppose it wouldn't be hard to sell this place."

"Whoa there, that's too fast—what if you hate how I live? What if you can't stand living in the country?"

"If I hadn't had dreams of living in the country for more years than I can count, and if I didn't think that this arrangement would work, then I wouldn't agree to leave this town."

"You still have to think about all the details, don't you? I mean, deal with your children, your friends, your practice?"

"Yeah, I do. Let's say that we have a tentative contract which hasn't been signed yet!"

"OK, Mrs. Lawyer, you come to Kerhonkson for an inspection visit and I'll make sure you love living like a mountain woman."

"It's my dream, you know. Please don't wake me up!"

Chapter 6
CONFRONTING THE COUNTRY COTTAGE

I arrived at the airport in Albany with my mind made up. No matter how creaky the old house was, or how remote the location, I knew that I was going to be married as surely as I knew that I hated being alone, unloved, remote from nature in a subdivision made of concrete walks and cookie-cutter residences, and needy to the point of desperation. I was a woman who had to try again for that lasting relationship that had eluded me. During my week at the home of my new sweetheart of old, little seemed to get in the way of my plans. I had developed a technique for ignoring obstacles, even if it meant resorting to wishful thinking.

✳✳✳

"I'm purposely taking you through the mountainous area," he admitted to me as we zigzagged along the circuitous Shawangunk pass from the Thruway to County Route 3."

"It's beautiful. But was there another way to get to the house?"

"Sure, I could have gotten off at Kingston, but that way you wouldn't have been impressed."

"Why not?"

"Just trust me—that route's not as impressive."

"Oh, OK. Are we almost there?"

"Here's our neighborhood now."

We made a sharp-angled nearly backwards turn into a narrow two-lane hilly road which dipped steeply and soon went across a bridge where the pedestrian walks had been marked "closed, due to construction." He waved out the window as we approached a stoplight where two competing gas stations, kitty-corner from each other, were facing two boarded-up businesses.

"This is downtown," he pointed out with his usual sarcasm.

"I guess it's not rush hour."

"Wait till you see our spread—you'll think you died and went to hillbilly heaven."

We reached the driveway that led up to the rear of the house in another ten minutes. As soon as we parked the car and emerged, he unlocked the back door and led me inside to the brightest yellow kitchen I had ever seen. The man who loved me had the Formica® counter straddling the radiators all set with luncheon dishes and flatware on paper napkins. He had planned to woo me with beautiful kisses, poetic words and a meal of sweet potatoes and wild pheasant. It was not under glass, but I accepted the wooing enthusiastically. He was right about the heaven part.

❊❊❊

The next morning he informed me that he had a few chores to attend to and that I should walk around the grounds.

"Just watch where you step," he warned. The neighbors' cats and dogs come around whenever they feel like it."

"It's wonderful here, honey. The air is so fresh and it's so very quiet!"

Just then a police siren sounded in the distance and a squad car flashed by on the highway. There were a couple of explosions down the road that reminded me of a detective movie in progress. He watched as my expression turned from dreamy to startled.

"I could have sworn those noises were shots, or something!"

"It's the end of hunting season—don't worry. After tomorrow, things will calm down. The police car was probably after some clod with an expired license plate or a noisy muffler. The shots you heard actually came from the woods behind the houses."

"Who's worried?"

He went into the garage at the far end of the driveway while I prepared to take a tour of the property. I had thought of it as an estate from the description in one or more of his letters, but now, as I saw it with my own eyes, I had to alter my perception a bit. It resembled a secluded thicket that extended all the way uphill, interrupted by a bulldozed plateau for people. There, amid all the towering ash, oak and maple trees, was the sweet little two-story house nestled on a hill facing the county highway. "So this is the place where I might be spending the rest of my life," I said to myself as I checked out my fiancé's carefully mowed crab grass. In the early morning light I thought the frame house had a solitary, almost haunted, look about it, yet it appealed to me in a primitive way. I couldn't explain it, but it seemed to be calling out to me to give it some attention. A scene from the movie, Green Mansions[1], flashed momentarily.

I didn't always have a camera hanging around my neck in those days, but the recollection of my first visit to my future Kerhonkson home will linger on in my mental pictures. I can almost hear the tree frogs shrieking..... .

✲✲✲

Dead leaves are swirling around and smell like Halloween, but the temperature is wrong. It feels more like summer and I'm happy as a young schoolgirl just dismissed from the final class before vacation. Before I begin round one of love nest inspection, I remove my jacket and wrap it around my waist. Now I am standing and staring at the eighty-five-year-old Cape Cod style cottage. It was originally built as a guest house on a chicken farm, but that doesn't explain why the trees and omnipresent weeds surrounding it have become overgrown to jungle-like density. Branches that have extended their forked limbs in all directions in order to compete for available sunlight now nearly obscure the view of the front porch. I take a closer look and see that it needs obscuring with its flaking paint and deteriorating floorboards. It is not inaccessible, however. A makeshift clearing through the tangle of growth has been hacked out. It leads down a set of rusted iron steps to a pile of firewood stacked next to the brick railing on one side, while a second clearing leads in the opposite direction to an enormous ash pile pressing against the other side of the railing.

This residence I am seeing is not consistent with my fairy tale images. I had always thought that the facade of a white wood-sided country house should be freshly painted and garnished with towering hollyhocks and colorful snapdragons. I could also envision some evergreen shrubs, petunias, zinnias and several strategically placed sunflowers to add a bit of diversity. There should have been a hanging basket of fuscias descending from the gabled roof over the front porch and mandatory wind chimes dingling intermittently, but they're not here. Instead, there's an unoccupied bird's nest wedged under the porch roof. Old droppings litter the small benches. Oh well, a woman's touch could fix this mess in a few good weeks.

I walk from where I am standing all the way to the rear of the house because there is no shortcut path enabling me to ascend from the front landing to the broad hill on the east side. Atop a flat area there, but unseen from the front yard, a pool has been installed. That entire sloping hill is also overgrown and besieged with brambles, mullein and prickly thistles. However, there is a narrow path from the back door, which has become the "grand entrance", leading to the eastern portion of the property where one can now observe a good-sized in-ground swimming pool. It lies in wait for the resumption of human activity, but this unfortunate former aquatic paradise is sadly neglected.

Since I am firm in my decision to enter wedlock with my starry-eyed widower, I accept his situation and his dedication to thrift. Nevertheless, I survey my future homestead with eyes that have spent the last fifteen years buried in high end living magazines. I counsel myself: "This is not high end living—at least until I get my hands on it."

The greenish water in the pool is choked with algae and other forms of life. If I stand and look into the water for a few minutes, I know I will see a telltale poke from below and then an expanding ripple of concentric circles indicating a presence of something alive. While I wait for my fiancé to finish chopping part of a cord of wood nearby, I scan the area around the pool and visualize how I will dig it all up and start over. Suddenly he creeps up behind me and doesn't say a word, but proceeds to embrace me with extreme familiarity.

"I'm looking at the pool," I demur.

"I can see that."

"There's something down there. I think it's a sea monster."

"It's not the Loch Ness and it aint Puff the Magic Dragon. It's fucking frogs."

"Is that what they're doing?"

Ignoring me, he goes on: "I was going to fill in the pool with dirt from the field up the hill."

"Why would you do that?" I query, staring into his face, searching for a spark of ambition.

"Nobody uses it any longer. Keeping it clean is a part-time job."

"What about me? I like to swim—it's good exercise!"

He stares at my shape and permits his eyes to travel down the line where my waist begins and my hips flare out in noble proportions. Yes, I'm a Botticelli woman, all right, and I've just let loose of a morsel of bait to see if he bites.

"You don't know what you're talking about. The chemicals are corrosive to your hands—you have to take frequent readings—ahhh, I just don't see you doing that kind of grunt work!"

"Bringing the pool back to life will enhance the value of the property!" I am attempting to ring up a pretty good sale, but like an inexperienced marketer of my strengths, I can't quite close the deal.

"Maybe I'll let you try, but I still think I'll wind up doing all the work."

"How will you manage to fill in the pool, if you choose to do that?"

"Bulldozer."

"Does that mean you'll do it yourself?"

"Of course not. I'd get Arnie to do it."

"Oh, well if you really do that, I'll probably be upset."

He looks into my eyes, searching for a spark of ambition. At that point I stop talking about it—not because I have wised up, but because he has suddenly heard the phone ring inside the house and has left the poolside. My thoughts continue to race on with resolute fervor. "Gee whiz," I think, "if Claudette Colbert could adapt to the life of a hick in that movie, "The Egg and I,"² so can I." Feeling stronger with every moment of my wishful thinking, I walk back into the house, determined to make the giant leap from high heels and anklets to rubber gloves and kneepads.

✳✳✳

I became officially engaged seated on a worn sofa in his small living room, with my intended seated next to me and an enormous caribou mount right above our heads as witness. We toasted our union with some vintage wine he brought up from the cellar. I watched as he first breathed in the aroma and then drank heartily while never removing his gaze from mine. He soon drained his glass, while I sipped slowly, being a woman who has never appreciated alcoholic beverages. Across from the sofa was a generously sized wood stove which gave the entire room a charcoal smell as the sounds of burning logs inside its belly provided the required ambience for a love nest. I regarded our engagement ceremony as I would regard a scene out of a western movie. I loved western movies.

✳✳✳

He returned to my town house the following month as my fiancé. We discussed the many details of my move to his domain as though we were old marrieds planning to relocate from the family residence to a vacation house. I thought of it as my retreat and I'm not sure if he shared my optimism one hundred percent, but he seemed pretty happy. Then he left again, saying goodbye with a passionate embrace and a gleam in his eyes. As he made his departure to attend to his ongoing life, I sat quietly by myself on the love seat in the loft of my town house where I had spent more hours of sad contemplation than I cared to recount.

Annie called soon after my return. "Well?" That was all she had to ask.

I bubbled over with nouns, verbs and an assortment of descriptive clauses. "What irony," I began, as I told my dear friend of my discoveries, fears and decisions. "You know how I bought this townhouse?"

"Yes, you've done an enormous job of furnishing it—it's gorgeous! Plus, it has my paintings. I guess the Mickey Mouse piece represents the entry into your life of a former animation artist. It's cute and he's cute!"

"I think so too, but remember, we're talking about this peach-colored castle with a mortgage. I spent three years and thirty thousand dollars I didn't have making it my dreamland. It might only take me ten years to pay off all the credit card bills."

"I thought you were doing well in your law practice."

"I am. But I probably went overboard and gussied this place up a little too soon. I think my purchase of all this art and antique stuff—forgive me, your work is a delight and it goes to the country with me—all these purchases were made to stave off my loneliness. And now, of course, I have to empty it all out and put the house on the market."

"So? As long as I've known you, you've done what you had to do."

"What else can I say? Now I finally realize that the loveseat I'm sitting on while talking to you has been a security stand where I've dealt with my frustrations. Sarah tried to turn me into a Science of Mind believer, but she forgot to deal with my hormones! It took me a long time to decide to marry this guy, like at least twenty-four hours! I said yes because I had to. Saying no would have undone years of fantasizing!"

"In your case, several decades!"

"Yes, I've gotten damned tired of relying on substitutes for male affection while being proselytized."

"She's after me too. Listen, I dig male affection. Only it often comes with some bad karma that you discover after it's too late."

"Annie, in this world, you make your own karma. I'm going to marry this dude and love him until he melts like an M and M® in my hand."

"You've got the commercial wrong—M and M's don't melt in your hand."

"You see—I don't even have time to watch TV commercials! Now, I'll be a lady of some leisure!"

Conversations with my dear friend always had an effect on me, sometimes kicking in long after I had hung up the phone. My head was filled with a mixture of glee, sexual anticipation and wonderment. I was pulling off a big life game-changer. Was it an accomplishment or an escape? What if it was both? Had I had enough of Illinois? What would happen to my law practice? Instinctively, I knew I had acted in my best interests. A loving marriage was more important to me than a loving relationship with architecture and bric-a-brac. I knew I could do some tax business from afar, even if it involved some traveling. So what was the big deal? My parents and brother were deceased and I had long ago dealt with the details of their passing. What could turn out to be the bump in the road?

Oh yeah, the kids. I would be leaving the home state of my entire brood, not to mention all my friends. I could always make new friends, but I surely wasn't going to make more kids. Well, I reasoned, life goes on. When did anybody ever get a guarantee that a momentous decision was the right one?

Chapter 7
THEY DON'T GET TO VOTE

Although I had informed my three children that I was in a new serious relationship, I hadn't given them all the details yet. Now I was ready to spring the news about my moving to Upstate New York. My daughter would be the easiest to handle, since she actually remembered him as a funny character who drew cartoons. Actually, I <u>had</u> seen my new fiancé since high school—there had been a visit from him a few years after his first marriage. He and his wife came to call on us as friends when my daughter was eight years old. When I phoned her with the news of our engagement, she had blurted out:

"Oh, I remember him! Wasn't he the guy who drew that cartoon of a character drawing a character inside the drawing, and then more characters inside that? It was like a Chinese box, because you kept seeing things inside things! What happened to his wife?"

"She died."

"So it was the class reunion thing. Wow!"

"Well, honey, what do you think?"

"I think if you love him. then it was meant to be."

It was amazing to me that she had a clear recollection of that visit. My two sons were then six and four and neither of them had any memory of meeting him. Although my daughter was a romantic type and believed in fate, my opinion was that none of my children had a true sense of why I had suddenly decided to marry again. Perhaps it was because they were my children. My older son was less understanding.

"Mom, I thought you were going to stay here until you got old. You have a business and you have us. How will we get to discuss things?"

I looked at this young man who had been through a lot with me during my two marriages and my several trial relationships. "I think we'll be closer than ever because my feelings of guilt will make me pick up the telephone more!"

"Well, Mom, I want you to be happy. What can I say? He's a real good guy, isn't he?"

"He's my kind of man. I do love him."

"What about his money? You said he's retired. It's OK for me to ask, isn't it?"

"Yes, it's OK."

"Well?"

"He can live on his savings. I'm still going to do long distance work. We'll be fine."

I was spouting these words with all semblance of confidence, but in the recesses of the maternal confines of my mind, I did worry that the poor little tykes, ages 30, 32 and 34, wouldn't be able to manage very well without me around to remind them to take their vitamins, watch out for strangers or pay their bills.

The apron strings were tough to cut, but I knew I had to sever the bonds of dependency. I hadn't suddenly gotten over my tendency to baby them, however. I figured they would manage well enough, but would I? I needed a big dose of courage because if anyone was enabling somebody else, I knew in my gut where the arrow of culpability was pointing—right at me! I had been much too protective with my children and especially so with my younger son. He was the one who pleaded with the most obstinacy: "Mom, you had two husbands already, including Dad! Can't you stay put and stay single?"

"Mind your own business, kid. Get a better job. Save some money. I'll call you once in awhile to be sure you're breathing regularly. Oh, and get your teeth looked at."

"You're not leaving town, really, are you?"

"Does this wedding invitation to our party on the outskirts of East Bumblefuck, New York, look like I'm kidding?"

"You shouldn't swear, Mom—what's the real name of the town you'll be moving to?"

"Kerhonkson."

"Gazundheit."

"Thanks. Don't bother to write. Just get your car oiled up before you make the trip from Chicago."

"I'm not making any trip. And what makes you think I don't take care of my car? "

"I don't know—it always sounds funny. Maybe you just drive funny."

48

"I'd love to trade it in for a new model—I don't guess you'd want to loan me ten thou? Naah, I'm sorry I brought it up. I can see you making faces already."

"I don't have ten thou. I don't even have minus ten thou—Remember? I ran up my credit cards to fix up my new townhouse!"

"Yes, but now you'll be selling it at a loss—what sense is that?"

"Love means never having to make sense or borrow."

"You mean he has money, don't you?"

"I don't know. He has twenty-one and a half acres and thousands of trees."

"You can't live in the country. You can't even mow your own lawn. What about your law practice?"

"I'm taking it with me. I have a computer, a telephone, a fax and there's Fed-Ex. Who needs to pay rent on a big office? I'll be fine."

"OK. But I'm mad at you. I'm never going to call you again. Just lock the door from the inside on your way out. I'm not even going to get up from this sofa to say good-bye."

"Gee, I see you're grateful for all that I've done for you. I gave you life and you're giving me the door."

"What did my brother say? He's the least independent, you know."

"He told me he would miss me and seemed to have a strange look in his eyes."

"Well, he is strange—you know that. What did the sister think?"

"She's happy for me."

"Yeah, she would be. She's so scatterbrained she has no clue."

"She's OK—she has her own life."

My younger son was never going to accept anything I did, so I gave up trying to change his attitude. Still, I had to admit to myself that I was the mother leaving her little birds who did not always have the knack of flying down pat. There would be my reservations about the arrangement, but I'd have to deal with it. "I'm doing the right thing for me," I rationalized. In one last burst of enabling frenzy, I arranged for them not to have to travel to Upstate New York in order to experience the nuptials. We scheduled <u>two</u> wedding receptions—one for my crowd in Chicago and one for his in the faraway hills. We decided to get hitched in Illinois first because most of the guests were my clients and I could write off some of the cost of the party.

✳✳✳

The Chicago wedding reception, held after our more intimate marriage ceremony, was a big happy afternoon affair with a huge two-tiered cake. The cake had been provided by the banquet hall as part of the menu, but there was a joke in the center of it. Someone had surprised us and found a photo of the two of us from our high school prom and inserted that snapshot of us as teen-agers atop the upper tier. We didn't look like that any longer. My husband had sported a great head of hair with a huge well-greased wave right out of the fifties and I could have been taken for twelve years old—resembling a flower girl with my tulle gown over full crinolines. I tried not to reflect on the fact that it was the third time that some of the attendees were celebrating my marriage.

After the party we returned to my townhouse and entertained my groom's family with a supper and cocktails. It was the last time I would be walking on high piled carpeting instead of a practical tweed rug laid over an old wooden floor. The next morning, while we were loading up a rent-a-truck, we had our first fight over my electric can-opener. The conflict had to happen and we passed that hurdle. Soon everything was stashed in the truck and we took off like two middle-aged remarrying folks always do—bringing our baggage with us.

When I look back on that first day on the road, I have to laugh. Neither of us could remember if I had locked the front door to the now empty townhouse. I began to fret, worrying about it. He tried to comfort me.

"What's in the house that anybody can steal?"

"I don't know—maybe the appliances—I don't know."

"I'll call the local police and tell them to be on the lookout for a washing machine. Did you remember to take out the wet clothes?"

"What do you think I am? An empty head?"

"I would never say that about you. But as a precaution, maybe you should inform the real estate agent. Say, did you really sell all your fancy office outfits?"

"I did."

"Good. You may not remember this, but there's very little closet space for your clothes in our house."

"I do remember, and I'm glad you said "our" house and not "your" house. That's a good sign. I have only five suitcases and two garment bags of things to wear."

"Five suitcases and two garment bags of what? You just said you sold your office outfits."

"Oh, I didn't sell my nice going-out clothes or my summer stuff or my sportswear—just the courtroom lawyer outfits."

"Oh, just the courtroom outfits. Wait a minute—you hardly ever go to court—you told me you do most of your work from your office!"

"I do. That's why it was so easy for me to get rid of the tailored clothes I hardly ever wore."

"I think I understand. You apparently still have a city girl wardrobe. We'll have to figure out what to do with those suitcases and the rest. My daughter hasn't moved her stuff out of her room yet, and that's where your things will have to be stored."

"Oh. When is she going to? And what do you mean, 'stored?' "

"I meant to say 'placed gently with loving precision.' I don't know when she's moving her stuff out. Every time I ask her she says, "Whenever.""

My brand new husband got into the driver's seat of the U-Haul, while I got into the driver's seat of my Ford. Being loved was more important than being well-dressed. We drove East in our little caravan of togetherness, new husband waiting for the pleasures of a new wife, or so I'd hoped, and me waiting for the other shoe to drop. I never looked back even once at the old silos along the Calumet River as Illinois faded into the distance. I was ready to live my newly invented life as a shit-kicking, truck-driving country woman with a whole new attitude.

As I followed along behind him, worshipping this guy who was taking me away from it all, I felt something ominous on my right hand. Oh crap, I had broken a fingernail.

Chapter 8
PIG ROAST FOR THE LOVERS

Our second wedding reception took us to the hills of Ulster County, a few miles down the road from our house, where I was assured that in our part of the countryside the number of cows outnumbered the number of humans. En route to the big party, I asked my beaming husband, happy as a dog returning to his favorite hearth by the fireplace, the following question: "When they post these signs for population, do they cheat?"

"Why do you think that?" Mr. Rustic inquired.

"Because I don't see any people here—we've been driving for three miles to get to the gun club reception and all the houses by the road look sort of abandoned."

"Oh, honey, they're not abandoned—it's just that some of the residents along this particular county route haven't gotten around to painting their siding for awhile. Also, you're accustomed to seeing cars in driveways. Here they keep their tractors and pickups in the barns or behind the outbuildings."

"We just passed a big farm-looking place where I saw a sign that said "Maple Sirup" for sale—they spelled it 'S I R U P!' Don't these people know how to spell?"

"They don't need to know spelling, dear. The family that owns that farm could buy and sell us and other people you know three times over—they have over a thousand acres of prime corn-growing land. One part of that property runs along the Rondout Creek, which makes it worth more than you can believe."

"Gee, I wish I had brushed up on the law on riparian rights or that IRS form 1040F for farmers before we got here."

"Reparian? Does that have anything to do with fixing things?"

"I said 'RI PARIAN,' silly, it means the legal rights of land-owners along river banks."

"I knew that—one of the guests you will meet this afternoon has many acres along that creek and he's always talking about it. He's a bit innovative—when he needs a waterfall to add to the am-bience of his property, he hires a crew to dynamite the rocks along the Rondout to alter the course of the flow of water. The town seems to have an issue with that."

I'd like to meet that guy!—he sounds like my kind of nature lover!"

"That's good. You'll like him, but maybe not as a potential cli-ent—as an entertaining friend. He hates to pay lawyers anyway—he gives favors instead."

"Favors? Like what?"

"Well, he'll dig up a sugar maple tree for you if you like and have it trucked over to our front yard."

"Who plants it?"

"That's not his problem."

"I'll stick to the social part, and I promise not to pitch my legal expertise right away. Besides, he sounds like a guy who needs a defense lawyer. I'm an income tax specialist, you know."

"Good luck getting tax business. Around here it's quite amazing how few customers there are who will admit to having income."

With that, I quieted down, having dismissed my previous real estate experience as something I wasn't particularly keen about. I was anxious to meet my husband's groupies, however. We approached the landmark edifice where the Kerhonkson Rod and Gun Club had built its own lodge. I was finally treated to the sight of real people in and around the place. Casual dress seemed to be the order of the day, with the men preferring jeans and the women in peasant blouses and full skirts. I whispered to my husband, even though a whisper wasn't required: "I think I'm overdressed."

"It's OK—that way everyone will know you're the bride."

✳✳✳

I had pictured our grand entrance in my mind several times. One of my favorite stories of all time was the novel, Rebecca[3], where the humble bride of low social standing meets the group of servants in her new husband's mansion. The twist to my anticipation involved my concern about being a second wife, marrying an established resident so soon after the first wife's passing. I thought I should practice being comfortable ahead of time, but our whirlwind activities prevented that.

"Honey," I began, "I thought that my introduction to my new neighbors was going to be cold turkey, but look, we're having hot pig."

"I told you about these pig roast caterers—doesn't that cooking smell great?"

"I didn't realize that they did all the cooking outside—right next to where the guests park—well, at least the weeds are mowed, even if all the muddy ruts sort of detract from the tidiness of the landscape."

"We've had a lot of late spring thunderstorms. You'll get used to it, but watch your shoes."

The setting was different from the banquet hall where we had entertained our Chicago-area guests. That building had a fine parking lot and fellows who rushed toward each arriving car to hand the driver a valet ticket, while this building had surroundings where the spent brass of handguns littered the ground amid seasoned animal poop. The club committee in charge of clean-up had made an attempt to beautify the immediate area where ladies who wore shoes instead of hunting boots would be walking up to the entrance. They had filled large flower pots with beautiful lilies and leafy silver dollar plants where the newlyweds could feel treated royally with touches of nuptial adornments.

I appreciated the effort that went into this event, which was handled far differently than the way an urban banquet establishment operated. These people who prepared the lodge were not paid for their services—they were volunteers who would be rewarded with thanks during the speeches scheduled during the serving of the dessert. I had been warned that the speeches would seem to go on forever and that many of the ladies brought books or knitting to deal with the tedium. Also, the dessert would not be served in parfait glasses with china plates—it would be served in soup bowls of homemade ice cream heaped with toppings spooned out by the wives of the members.

Since we had been married in Illinois, there was no need for a procession or a show of traditional vows. They got right to the hors d'Oeurves and beer. The hors d'Oeurves consisted of bacon rinds and fried dumplings, which were enjoyed as people stepped up to the buffet table—two appropriated reloading benches covered with floral oilcloths.

I had given myself time to bone up on the history of the place by reading one of my husband's paperbacks. Ulster County was an area where the Dutch settlers back in the 1600's first established their homesteaded farmland by virtue of grants from the British. We would be feted at an historic site where American freedom of expression began.

So there I was, freely expressing myself in the only way I knew how—wearing my black silk pants suit purchased years before from the old Bonwit Teller store on Palm Beach's Worth Avenue. I had adorned the shirt part with a diamond and pearl pin from Marshall Field near one collar and a gigantic orchid corsage on the other. My husband, the groom, was resplendent in his best and newest beige knit shirt with its pocket flap buttoned down to conceal an ironed but unstarched handkerchief, and his favorite pressed brown slacks. I knew that he carried his 22 somewhere on his person for protection, but I didn't necessarily remember where it was—only that his belt had a key role in addition to holding up his pants.

He had given me a list of the guests. Pruning this list to the number of people who could fit into the central room of the clubhouse was no mean task, since he had served as President of the organization in the past and had formed many close relationships. Most of the guests were couples, and it was impossible for me to keep track of all the names. They knew who I was, however—I was the "new wife." After several introductions where I was referred to by my smiling husband in a manner that was beginning to make me uncomfortable, I took him aside. "Honey," I said with the utmost care, "if you're going to keep introducing me as your 'new wife,' can I then refer to you as 'my latest husband?'" He got the message and we made a fresh start at introductions for the latecomers just arriving.

For anyone who has never enjoyed the dining experience of a genuine pig roast catered by a specialist in this category of cuisine, it's a real novelty. Unless you're committed to avoiding even an occasional splurge of high fat content fare, you'll probably ask for seconds. Some of the guests had thirds and fourths. I got to taste a yummy portion, but I was too busy shaking hands to total up the calories.

There was no central air conditioning system in the gun club on this particular steamy day at the beginning of June, but they did have window units that blasted out cold air from time to time. However, the gun club members were thrifty with their budgets and hadn't provided any backup systems for special events. Some of the guests, including me, got a little sweaty when the window units failed to operate while too many electric coffee makers were turned on.

The black silk shirt of my outfit was never the same after that because the temperature in the clubhouse dining room soon became the same temperature as the outside air right next to the huge pig roasting contraption. I wasn't sure what smelled more— the dripped pig grease or the underarms of the overheated guests. It was all in good fun and nobody seemed upset by the inconvenience. I kept my own thoughts to myself. Everyone seemed happy to be there except for one couple who spent the afternoon exchanging glares. I learned later on that they divorced a month after the festivities.

For our Chicago area reception I specifically wrote "no gifts please" on the invitations because we were not exactly a twosome starting out in life. We already had too much stuff between us. However, my husband-to-be told me that the Ulster County folks would be hurt if they couldn't bring gifts because that was their tradition. We received so many unusual presents that I ran out of the usual words of thanks. Country women love to knit, sew, raise flowers, do craft work and share their creations whenever the opportunity arises. I unwrapped knit toaster covers, assorted sizes of crocheted doilies with our monogram, a mammoth picnic basket set, decorated ceramic planters done in kilns by small children, five aprons with kitschy sayings and plaques that were most suitable for bathrooms. Since our cozy cottage was built shortly after indoor flush toilets had become the norm, with its typical small lavatory, I wondered where we were going to put all the plaques. Our country home was already overflowing with an abundance of artifacts and accessories.

After sixteen years of marriage we still haven't had the occasion to use our accumulated loot. I recall that the picnic basket ensemble sat in an obscure storage shelf in our cellar for years, completely neglected, although we often ate in parks and at rest stops during our travels. In a burst of enthusiastic household reorganization one day, I discovered that the toaster covers and doilies had disappeared into thin air. Somebody had been disposing of items that were never put to use, and that somebody surely wasn't me.

Someone took photos of everybody and the photographer waited with his camera until most of the beer had been consumed. I put all those prints in an album and I can still pick out which of the guests went overboard by reference to how chummy the men got with the women in the poses. After assessing the two contrasting receptions I had to admit that the one in the country had tastier food, a friendlier atmosphere and more memorable moments. The most vivid moment occurred when the toilet facilities inside the clubhouse proved inadequate for the crowd and those guests with the most urgent needs found relief in the wooded area next to the shooting range. My introduction to the rural lifestyle had begun.

Chapter 9
TRYING NOT TO GET LOST IN ANOTHER AMERICA—PART ONE

When I recall my first visit to the Kerhonkson house, just prior to our engagement, one vivid fact stands out for me—I never gave much attention to the <u>inside</u> of the dwelling itself—I only had eyes for its occupant. OK, the vivid yellow enamel paint on the walls, the yellow counters and the spacious yellow refrigerator did catch my eye, but otherwise I simply dismissed the decor in all the other rooms as a trivial matter that could be addressed later.

"What do you think of my house?" he asked me as soon as I had been treated to a fifteen-minute tour.

"It's adorable. It's got everything. It's got you."

"What's your favorite part?"

"The outside, I think."

"You mean the exterior?"

"I mean the views from all the windows. Let's go outside again—I have to be certain that I voted correctly."

We exited via the back door next to the kitchen and gazed at the colors of the clouds as they filtered the effects of the setting sun with a breathtaking display. How could I not notice the beauty of the mountain views from both the Southwest and the Northeast? What could be more romantic than a loving partner gesturing enticingly against a backdrop of a rural sunset?

After our marriage and my settling in, I excitedly planned a succession of explorations. He had suggested new hiking boots for me to replace my Birkenstocks. I relished my private nature walks—excursions into our own private ravine, where I discovered an area that had served as a hidden dumping ground for discarded equipment and broken tools. But that was just the beginning. I examined an old foundation on the property near the road. A portion of what had been a brick stairwell was still attached to it, so I guessed I was viewing all that remained of a former brick residence. As happens with all abandoned structures, the seeds already in the ground—the ones which had never given up waiting for their chance to take over—now had taken over. Sprouts had become saplings and those roots that understood that a concrete foundation posed no problem now grew into trees. I decided to go on a fact-finding mission, using my husband, the property owner, as a source.

"Honey, tell me about that foundation with the tree roots and the growing stuff all over it."

"There was a main house on the property long ago. It burned down."

"Oh, maybe there's a story there! Who lived there?"

"People. Now only wild animals and plants. Anything else you need to know?"

"Yes, why is an old wheelbarrow and a push mower and a couple of rotten bookcases lying behind the trees near the back of that strip of land?"

"Why <u>are</u> an old wheelbarrow and a push mower, etc. Don't use the word 'is' when there are more subjects than one."

"Are you kidding?" What about my question?"

"Oh, we had no further use for those objects, so they were placed there for a future art project."

"I don't believe you—you just threw them there because you were too busy to, uh, to whatever you do with old things."

"What did you do in Chicago with old things?"

"Oh me, well when my mother died I put all her stuff in my garage and then I gave it away to the Salvation Army."

"OK, you have my permission to give that stuff from my unused art project away. We can use the tax deduction!"

"I can't lift those things! There's weeds and saplings growing all over the stuff!"

"And Mrs. Lawyer slash explorer slash enquiring reporter, what happens to old man-made objects that get grown over by nature?"

"Oh, I can answer that—they become artifacts and eventually the archaeologists dig them up and learn about prior civilizations!"

"That's right! You've got it! Send in the archaeologists! But I suggest you wait at least another hundred years!"

"I get it—you're being practical. Well, I'll try to remember that aspect of your personality, now that it's too late for me to exchange the plain gold wedding band for a new cocktail ring."

It dawned on me early in our marital relationship that I was being referred to by my husband's friends as "a change of pace." This concerned me. I decided to consult with some of the wives in our neighborhood with whom I had become somewhat friendly. "Tell me," I would ask," what was my husband's deceased wife really like?" This query could have been taken right from Daphne Du-Maurier also, but I really needed to know. The answers I received from several women were starkly similar:

"She was very nice—on the quiet side."

Or, "I got along well with her—she was soft-spoken."

The topper was, "She didn't talk a lot, but she was a very good listener. You knew she was paying attention to you when you spoke."

I digested the results of my research grudgingly. Now I knew what I was up against. My true love was not only painfully practical; he couldn't deal well with my verbosity. I was raised in a family of interrupters and it had rubbed off on me, like an indelible stamp. I recalled one of my mother's friends using my name and the term "magpie" in the same sentence. The man I had married was so interesting to me when he spoke that I couldn't contain myself. However, he couldn't take it when I butted in while he was finishing a sentence.

"Let me finish!" he would insist, casting a stern expression my way. My problem was that I was never quite certain when his sentence or sentences were completely over. If I had something to say which I considered pertinent, I would forget what it was when I thought it might finally be my turn to speak. I still have a problem in this area today, except that over the years I have developed a sort of crust. To my delight, I discovered that he did it to me too, and I now enjoy informing him of that fact.

One afternoon, while I was still in my bubbling over mode of small talk, I was given a demonstration. Instead of his resorting to the usual stern look or a hand signal which he had begun to employ, he calmly folded his newspaper, the reading of which I had interrupted, and retired to his private study in the downstairs bathroom. This single move was a genuine wallop to my ego. He had built shelves for books across from the toilet, which meant he was unlikely to run out of reading material. I felt so deflated that I resolved to come to terms with our differences. First, I forced myself to accept the fact that he had married me for better or for worse and that I had gone along with it. Second, I convinced myself that he was a contemplative sort who needed his space. I promptly renamed the bathroom a "hygiene library." That recharacterization made me feel better when I felt temporarily abandoned, which had become a frequent occurrence.

I soon figured out that I did sound a bit like a pest, so, as part of my learning curve on how to get along with a pragmatist spouse of quiet demeanor, I rewired my brain to reinforce my new understanding—sometimes he had to do his thing his way while I had to do my thing my way. It was about then that I decided to return to my botanical discovery project and take his advice by wearing my new clunky boots.

"This place is fun", I thought, as I mapped out new paths on which to wander the following day.

He always asked me about my work. "Don't you have some client obligations to handle?"

"Yes," I always replied, "I took care of them early this morning—my tax season has wound down to a trickle."

"Maybe you'd like to do some accounting or legal work out here?"

"Sure—ask some farmer if he needs his chickens recounted. I could do an audit of his feeding equipment and grain supplies."

"I meant do some real estate or estate planning."

"I finished my application for a New York law license. I'm waiting for the certification."

"You don't sound motivated."

"I'm motivated to meet people and see what they're up to. That's how I get clients. As soon as the reciprocity paperwork is handled, I'll put an ad in the Yellow Pages."

We were just babbling at the time, but a little cloud of mystery and half-truth hung over our personal atmosphere. I had been a city tax lawyer handling specialized matters of urban clients. Things were done differently here in a different county in a different state. I couldn't quite confide in him yet that I wasn't about to reinvent myself as a generalist. I knew the truth—I just didn't like it. My expertise didn't quite fit in with the local culture.

Finally, my New York law license had been activated, so I needed to make some professional decisions. My first decision was to confront my husband with the situation:

"Dear, I see that the local folks here have different needs than my clients in Chicago. That ad I put in the paper for a lawyer? I got a call from a logger who lives a few miles away—he needed someone to defend his son for driving drunk."

"How much can you charge for representing the drunk?"

"I never did that kind of work. I'm an estate planning specialist!"

"Well, some of these landowners here—they have lots of money. Why don't you plan their estates?"

"Good idea. But you forgot what my ad said—it said I was concentrated in the fields of tax and estate work. The guy that called said he had somebody for that already. His son was a no-good trouble-maker who probably could use a hard-nosed woman lawyer to get him out of scrapes."

"Sounds like a profitable line of work. Try it."

"I'm too old to get into an entirely new field. Besides, trouble-shooting doesn't fit my personality!"

"Oh yes it does. You're a natural. You can talk your way through anything."

"I would have to go to Albany and learn court procedure here."

"OK, I see the problem. I've got a job for you. The township needs a person to fill a vacancy on the real estate tax appeal board. Go get it!"

And that's how I became a part-time real estate tax special-ist. It was very part time—like six weeks out of the year. My actual work schedule had diminished greatly. However, I saw an upside: Less time spent at my computer meant more time for me to hike and gape. The poet and nature lover in me came out of hiding and confronted the tax attorney in me. For the time being the poet and nature lover held sway. I had brought many books with me—some were field guides about trees and wild flowers.

What would he think if I spent more time in the woods than at my computer? "Oh honey," I began, "I'm caught up with my legal work, so I'm going to go exploring today."

"I thought you did that already."

"Listen, exploration isn't a one or two-day project. How long did it take Columbus to figure out that the earth was round and then later on that the New World didn't have spices?"

"Uh, I don't know. You're not Columbus. How are you going to afford exploration paraphernalia if you're not collecting fees?"

"Easy. I'm not buying any more stuff—All I need is hiking boots and a pad and paper."

"You? Not buying stuff? That's about as reliable a prediction as the world being flat."

"You think I can't change my habits?"

"People don't change."

And that was the end of that discussion. He went back to reading a book about military history and I went out in our woods again, rationalizing my lack of serious gainful employment. I had put him on notice that I was about to have fun by simply wandering around looking for specimens. What good were field guides if they just sat in a box somewhere? I went for some long walks which I characterized as a form of therapy. But I didn't merely walk my new premises harboring poetic thoughts of flora and fauna—I floated. It was too bad I only floated figuratively and not actually, because real floating, like Wendy and the boys did in Peter Pan, did not require hiking boots. We could have saved some money.

Chapter 10

TRYING NOT TO GET LOST IN ANOTHER AMERICA—PART TWO

As the first weeks of our new life together passed, our conversations became easier and more light-hearted, especially when I watched his lip movements carefully. He would ask, "What did you do this afternoon?"

"I walked up to the orchard and looked for apples. I invented a new dessert. You can check it out tonight."

"You actually found apples? It's a bit early in the season. They must be very small."

"That's why I had to invent a new dessert. No wonder most of the apples were so green. I saw a few late-blooming flowers screaming for attention and edible wild blueberries growing in the scrub. So without enough real apples, I filled in the pastry with canned apple slices and wild blueberries. Oh, and I am decorating the serving dish with yellow flowers. It will go with the kitchen."

"Sounds great to me. I know that dish will be tasty—especially the dandelions."

"Not dandelions, dummy, wild celandine—from the family *Papaveraceae*."

"You do that and you'll have to clean it up."

"What?"

"Oh, I hate to spoil your mood, but I could have guessed where you went. You must have stepped on something—there's crap all over the floor."

I raised my right leg to examine the treads of one of my hiking boots. He was right. "I'll clean the floor up—it must be some kind of animal droppings."

"Are you surprised? All kinds of animals roam around up at the orchard."

"I thought no animals were allowed up there! What were all those "Posted" signs doing there?"

"Oh, those were for all the animals that can read. They have an agricultural college out here!"

"Smart aleck! I meant the animal pets that owners take for walks—on leashes, I assumed."

"Leashes? You've got to be kidding! The 'Posted' signs are for trespassers who think they can hunt anywhere! You were walking on the turf of bears, rabbits, skunks, squirrels and deer. Did you think they were trained to look for an outhouse?"

"Don't continue—I get the message. Let me please clean the floor."

"I'll clean it. Go outside and hose off your boots."

I dutifully exited through the kitchen door and found the garden hose wound around a metal contraption. Just as I figured out which way to turn the balky handle to get the water going, the hose end turned on me and I ended up drenched. I knew he would razz me if I returned to the house to change outfits, so, after I cleaned off my boots, I decided to let the afternoon sun do its job. "This is the life," I thought to myself as I stretched out on the front steps, which I had personally freed from overhanging greenery with a pruner. Although I still had major blisters on my right hand, I was a determined human weed whacker. I loved being able to sit on a step and look at the landscape without feeling hidden. So what if I was a little wet now? I was happy. Nothing could get in the way of my idyllic thoughts of lazy afternoons of summer and the call of the wild as the seasons changed.

After the days became longer as the summer equinox approached, I got a call from my friend, Annie, who had some news for me.

"You're going to feel very sad at what I'm about to tell you," she began. I knew her so well that I anticipated something I didn't want to hear.

"It's about Sarah, isn't it?"

"You heard?" Annie was not surprised at how intuitive I could be.

"I knew she wasn't well. So what happened?"

"She was staying in her flat during the heat wave in Chicago—I'm sure your kids told you about it—well, she must have had a stroke or something. I guess she didn't have air conditioning, or maybe it was broken."

"Annie, get to the point—what happened?"

"When her landlord found her she had been dead for at least two days."

"Oh My God!" I couldn't breathe for a minute or two. "So that's why I didn't hear from her. I did call her a couple of weeks ago."

"Do you want to know what Glenda did? Of course you do. She paid for her funeral, the wake, a casket, everything. She had the obituary printed in the Chicago papers and also in Sarah's home town in Athens. There were about twenty people at the graveside."

"I would have come in, you know."

"I knew you would and I decided not to call you for that reason. You're a newlywed and it was all very sudden and I made that decision. I hope you're not angry."

"No, I'm not angry—just sad about the whole thing. She never accepted my marriage, and I felt resentment, but after awhile it didn't matter any longer. I'm happy here, you know."

"I'd like to visit you next month. Is there a chance you can put me up for a week?"

"A chance? I'd love it."

So Annie came to visit us as the first of my friends to be welcomed by me in my new household. I had boasted of my efforts to wrest some memorable planted areas out of the turmoil of all the wild growth and she seemed impressed. It didn't surprise me when I saw that she had brought her painting equipment, including her easel, and did some sketches of my emerging garden while we chattered about everything.[4] She was not in a relationship at the moment, but had a couple of interesting new men in her life. I asked her if she was getting commissions and she told me she had been in contract negotiations to do a massive series of tapestries for a Fortune 500 company. It was her biggest commission ever and we celebrated by going to High Falls and dining at the world famous De Puy Canal House. She also took a photo of me and the house which I will treasure always. I was standing on the front steps squinting and wearing a shocking pink tee-shirt. Even though I had partially cleared the area surrounding the steps, I was still nearly hidden in the picture behind the taller overhanging tree branches. I tell people who look at that photo that the pink thing in the middle is not a flower. Most folks stare for a moment and then recognize my face and my squint.

Annie's visit meant a great deal to me and was proof that I hadn't just forgotten all about my old friends. When it was time for her to pack up her stuff and take leave of us, I took her to the train station in Rhinecliff and sat with her while she waited for the train to arrive. As she and I walked over to the platform, I bid her goodbye and promised to see her when I got back to Chicago in the spring. I think we each cried and held each other for a considerable length of time.

✳✳✳

As I look back on those heady days of our first year, my reminiscences turn to some of the adventures along the way. I reminisce over the time that my husband worried I had become lost in the woods behind our house—he had searched for me for three hours and finally discovered me, huddling next to a rippling stream of gently rushing water that I was warned never to drink. It was nearly dark.

"Where the hell were you—didn't you take the compass?"

"Yes, but I couldn't see the dial."

"What did you do with the flashlight I gave you?"

"Oh, you mean this one with the spent batteries?"

"I told you always to take spare batteries."

"I'm sorry. Will you forgive me?"

"No. Let's go back to the house. I'll have to warm the dinner up for the fourth time."

"I'm freezing."

"You can sit in front of the wood stove. It's still hot because I put in more firewood."

"OK. Are you mad at me?"

"Yes, but I love you."

"I love you too."

I felt foolish as a child who has disobeyed as I threaded my way back to the house behind him. Single file trudging through the obstacles of the forest floor was the only viable method. I had already learned that wild growth forests do not contain uniform rows of neatly planted trees. I managed to avoid most of the bulkiest fallen limbs on the overgrown path—fungus encrusted specimens which had landed every which way, but I couldn't avoid stumbling over a rock that he seemed to step over like a seasoned woodsman. When we returned, he helped me get out of my thin jacket and noticed the new hole in my pants at the knee.

"You're bleeding."

"Oh, it's worse than that. I think I damaged my kneecap."

"You're walking—how bad could it be?"

"Huh?"

"Never mind. I'll tape it up. You're such a mess. Good thing I'm such a forgiving fellow."

"Yeah."

I recovered and my knee was OK and we were OK. Everything was OK. I even sewed a patch on my pants all by myself. Boy, had I changed. I thought my kids would never recognize me again, but they did, as they found time to visit us and explore my new world. They thought it was pretty neat. I patted myself on the back for being so brilliant because I was certain that nobody else would. After the last of my flock had left, I spent several hours sitting on the sofa in the small living room, cogitating about the deal I had cut and how happy I was. It was worth it, I gloated, as I removed most of my clothing in order to survive in the stifling heat of the massive wood stove that occupied half the small living room space.

Chapter 11

TO LOVE, HONOR, OBEY, PLUS CHANGE SOME BAD HABITS

I had to admit some painful truths about me—I kept bumping up against a resistance to change that showed up in my behavior. A particular session with a therapist years ago kept repeating itself in my head.

The therapist always began the sessions with the same question: "What's going on?"

I always had my standard answer: "I'm a nervous wreck." Then my eager voice of openness would spill out the usual gritty blather about why I had married two different husbands I could not stay married to and whether I was blind to my relationship weaknesses. The therapist took notes and even recorded the sessions. I actually packed each of the tapes in a box which I brought to Kerhonkson and intended to listen to them again when I felt overly courageous but needy. Fortunately or unfortunately, depending upon one's view of the value of therapy, the tapes had gradually deteriorated and I was never able to hear them.

However, I do have a very good recall of some of my concerns as my wedding day approached—my third. Therefore, I shall begin this piece of my drama with the point of no return—the wedding ceremony.

The nuptials were beginning and the rabbi was fashionably late. I already knew about those words I would be uttering in front of people who were already clued in about me. They make you say those time-tested vows and you're not allowed to be wishy-washy about it. But I had definite knowledge about these legal relationships, having been there: I knew those vows were incomplete. The new spouse, in his head, has filled in the blanks that the rabbi left out. It didn't take long for me to figure out that I had to shape up if I wanted my darling to remain nice to live with. This reflection is important, since it takes me back in time to a number of transitional situations where I had to cope in order to keep the fires burning.

Perhaps the most challenging for me involved my eating and fitness routines. I had been raised on Jewish cooking by a mother who tended to think in terms of appearances and wardrobes. Naturally, I had rebelled and determined for myself what suited my palate. Now enter into the equation an independent minded husband who had repeatedly claimed he had raised himself. No matter how many times I had questioned him about his childhood, the answer was always the same. "I was never a child."

This and other utterances forced me to construct my own version of his evolution: Judging from his lifestyle shifts and manner of speaking, I figured that nobody in his immediate family had ever dared to question his individualistic ways—especially his mommy or daddy. He had hinted that, due to his being the first grandchild, the entire clan had "spoiled him." I wished I had been similarly spoiled, but then our sparks would probably never have ignited as they did.

A typical conversation over one of our first breakfasts at the Kerhonkson house would have included undercurrents and subtleties suggestive of an odd couple. I recall a certain moment in our first summer together when my desire to please was destined to clash with my need for instant gratification.

✳✳✳

I am savoring the smoky taste of the two fresh fried eggs retrieved from the recesses of an old cast iron frying pan. I had noticed that my new mate's beat-up kitchenware reminded me of the contents of a back room in an antique dealer's cellar. "Honey," I venture, my lips revealing a remnant of yolk, so eager was I to extol his culinary virtue, "You are a really wonderful breakfast cook—but how did you manage to scrounge up this vintage set of pots and pans? It must have cost you a fortune!"

"No fortune. When I left home as a newly married I had my choice of a check from my folks, who had very little, or their old set of dishes and cookware. They were buying new pots and pans, so we took these. They've worked out."

"Well I never cooked in pots like these and I went to cooking school! Why I can barely lift the largest fry pan!"

"Poor baby with your weak city muscles. You're so accustomed to lifting legal files and thin briefcases. Want a suggestion to compensate for your lusty appetite? Why don't you take another run down the road with me tomorrow morning—only this time try a half mile instead of a ten minute warm-up."

"You mean try to keep up with you while you do your three mile jog? I <u>did</u> my share of running in my life! I used to run around the block several times back in Chicago. Out here there's no such thing as blocks—there's only, uh, frontage and steep switchbacks. Besides, you go too fast for me—I can't even sneak peeks at the neighbors' birdbaths or bushes to distract me from the misery!"

"Maybe stop peeking and start running."

"Surely you can hear me panting and see me straining at the bit?"

"I'll slow up next time, just to get you started."

"Maybe not today. Ask me again, please?" I hoped he would be patient with my lack of conditioning, as I reached for a third slice of toast.

He tried once more to make his case: "You know, gardening is a wonderful hobby, but driving to the local nursery and buying new plants doesn't quite use up as many calories as running or exercising on a regular basis."

"What about when I'm digging holes in the ground?"

"That would be useful if you performed a few pushups before each spadeful."

I downed a second cup of coffee, to which I had added more than one ounce of two percent milk and two spoonfuls of sugar. He had a point and I hated it. My reply sounded lame, even to me. "I plan to switch to skim milk and artificial sweetener." He seemed unimpressed, so I upped the ante. "I think my legs just can't compete with your legs. I'll try a smaller run on my own."

"I'm not trying to change you—I love you just the way you are. But you have gotten just a tiny bit cheekier since we got married."

"You left out the descriptive word 'plump,' on purpose, because you don't want to hurt my feelings."

"OK, I admit it. I'm seven inches taller than you, so I can eat two eggs and three slices of toast and not put on weight. But I also run three miles every morning."

"Give me a little time to adapt."

This trend of conversation seemed to pop up with increasing frequency until one day he presented me with a letter from a gym in Kingston congratulating me on becoming a new member. He waited for my reaction with suspense. I surprised him and even myself with my willingness to venture beyond my fear of pain and discomfort.

"I love the idea of going to a gym regularly!" I exclaimed. "It's just so, so, uh, practical."

"We'll go together. Then, after we work out, I'll take you to lunch."

"Lunch afterwards? Do you mean like a date? It sounds a tad like a bribe."

"It is a bribe."

"You're on." He had me right where he wanted me—a new inductee to fitness—a model of behavioral repudiation of fatness. I took on the challenge and entered into the program with less than one hundred percent devotion. In a few weeks I permitted one of the trainers to teach me about muscles and body fat measurement. After losing ten pounds and noticing that my blue jeans had become easier to zip up, I had to acknowledge that he was right about a lot of things. Still, he didn't know everything about me. I switched from breakfast toast to bagels after I discovered a great deli right near the gym. A little backsliding preserved my sense of stability. I wasn't quite ready for that much dedication.

Other old habits died hard as I began to lose my fear of assert-
ing myself and attempted to assume a firmer woman-of-the-house
role. I had always run my own show and now I had a husband
who was equally territorial. A showdown was soon in order and
the scene was set for me to rise up and take over—at least in the
kitchen. We didn't live in Mandalay and I wasn't going to let him
go on acting like the bossy Mrs. Danvers in the story of Rebecca.
The cast iron pots just had to go. I prepared for the skirmish by
finding a really great sale on kitchen ware and showed him the ad
for an anodized aluminum ten-piece set.

Skepticism on his part was a foregone conclusion. The expression on his face foretold his response, although I had to look
at him sidewise to see it because he was definitely avoiding eye
contact. Then came his predictable rebuttal. "We don't need it."

"I insist."

"You do? What don't you like about our cookware? It's made
to last forever."

"Forever is too long for me. Our food takes too long to heat
up and everything always sticks. I prefer lightweight and stick-free.
OK, so you volunteered to wash the dishes. I gave up my dishwasher when I married you, you know. At least let me have pots that are
more practical."

He finally grunted his approval and we bought a new set of
modern cookware and prepared to give away the cast iron stuff. As
I gathered up the collection carefully for donation, pure guilt over-
came me. I had gotten attached to the big stockpot. It was great for
stews and soups, so I kept it.

I had always prided myself at being adaptable, but as I im-
plemented each new phase of my transformation into the world
of country bumpkins, I continually suffered from emotional set-

backs. I knew that a psychologist would refer to this syndrome as a "loss." Surely I could forgive myself for clinging to some of my former idols, like central heating and air conditioning and two ovens—one for me and one for resale value. But there was a limit to my adaptability. I couldn't seem to accept the lack of closet space in the old house. My non-solution to my dilemma was handled ineptly, as I simply piled up my uncloseted outfits on a small dresser until they rose to an unstable height. He had a solution: "Get rid of any outfit you never wear." My solution was different. "Let's socialize more." The outcome of this dilemma was in his favor, however. I gave away five dresses and every last skirt and blouse I owned. Nobody dressed up in his social circle anyway—not even to go out to dinner. I didn't have a social circle.

I managed to dispense with my malaise over losing my status as clothes horse by immersing myself in local culture. I bought several books about the history of the Catskills and the seventeenth century Dutch settlement of upstate New York. My stepdaughter acquired a larger apartment and took her stuff out of the big storage area. I was finally moving in. The less I grumbled the better we got along. We seemed to cruise along in wonderful harmony that sizzled ever greater with each passing day. What could dampen this fervor when we each had such great attitudes, especially me? Then real life took over and little troubles began to put a brake on our momentum.

Winter came to the hills where our house was imprisoned between a mountain and a steep drop-off. Unending snow, ice and freezing winds arrived with it. We went to bed with our pavement and lawns showing and awoke in the morning to an all-white world. I would peer out the window to find evidence of life forms, but the sole giveaways that we weren't living somewhere near the North Pole were a few telltale sets of small animal tracks and birds' feet imprinted in the snow. They always seemed to lead from the far edge of the driveway to the opposite edge of the mowed area which we referred to as a lawn. I figured there was something out there greater than my somewhat self-centered mind had contemplated. I donned my heavy parka and tromped around like a kid looking for adventure. There were chickadees and acrobatic squirrels competing for seeds in the bird feeder. Tree limbs were groaning from gale force gusts while snow freshly plowed blew right back to where it originally lay—covering the driveway with inconvenient drifts. My husband, the weather master, had risen early to deal with the icy blacktopped area while I bustled around the kitchen gloating over my new lightweight frying pan. Then I heard a pounding on the door.

"Let me in—I've fallen!"

"What happened?"

"Oh, I slipped on the driveway and fell over a fucking bucket of calcium chloride! I think I've hurt some ribs."

"Don't move—I'll take you to the hospital!"

"No you won't—I'll call the doctor."

I heard him make an appointment on the phone. He drove himself to a medical center ten miles away and returned with the diagnosis. Three or four cracked ribs. Nothing to do but let them heal. He had some sort of wrap wound around his middle to prevent further injury. I wondered if he would acknowledge his vulnerability. He did it in his everyday macho manner.

"I'm going to the gym tomorrow. I'll stick to leg exercises for awhile."

I thought to myself, "Tough guy—he won't even let me take over the chores." I asked aloud, "Honey, how bad does it hurt?"

"Well, don't say anything funny for a few days."

"I promise. Uh, can you sit up OK in your favorite chair?"

"Yup."

"Can I get you some tea?"

"Only if you keep the teabag in and let it steep. I hate weak tea."

I thought to myself, "He hates anything that is weak, including the way I act sometimes." I decided not to pussyfoot around an idea that had been buzzing in me. "Can we talk about taking a winter vacation next year?"

"Absolutely." He was finally revealing a bit of a chink in that solid plate of armor he wore like a Roman soldier. Was this the beginning of Mr. Invinceable's vulnerability springing a leak? My heart reckoned it was time to thump. He continued, "One day I'm going to be too old to keep up this property, I guess."

I was witnessing something rare—a burst of humility from a wild child that rarely surfaced. I had cautiously rehearsed my painful decision to refrain from talking out of turn and wrecking the script. It worked because he continued to voice his previously unspoken idea. "We might consider getting a place in Florida."

It was finally the moment when I could speak. Words that I had strained to dam up within the confines of my motor mouth now poured out. "Oh, now that we've finally had all the huge ash trees leaning precariously over the roof chopped down and I've finally learned how to shovel the ice off the front steps without breaking my bones—now you realize that you're human?"

"Don't go crazy—I'm just considering the idea."

"Maybe I can buy a couple new pairs of slacks—that is, if the place you're simply considering has more than two closets!"

"You don't need more slacks. You do need to use the foot massaging gadget I bought for you. What did you do with it?"

Now why did he bring this up? Why now? "It's in the storage area."

"Why don't you use it?"

"My feet got better as soon as I opened the box."

"You're so stubborn!"

"Who, me?"

"No, I must have been addressing the dust on the tables you haven't gotten around to. You picked out that device after complaining endlessly. Why did I buy it?"

"You cared about my feet—I can't help it if they got better."

"The truth is, you glanced at the instructions and got nervous."

"The truth is, I read the instructions and couldn't figure out how to use the thing. It said something about assembling a part and I couldn't figure it out."

"Oh, now I understand. It was a stretch for your attention span."

"I'll go get it out of storage. I don't want to start an argument."

"Never mind."

"OK. You win."

Most of our arguments ended up a draw of sorts. Neither of us had the tenacity to pursue the merits of this or that widget versus the merits of his system of fitness measured against my hardcore resistance to mechanical detail or overly rigorous exercise. We were weary of bickering, slippery driveways and bitter cold Februaries. A warm climate seemed to beckon and we began taking winter vacations where no snowflake would dare to fall.

❋❋❋

Two years flew by. Now we were driving home from a restful two-week Florida vacation on a particularly cold February day. We reached the house and noticed that a fallen tree had blocked our driveway access. That was why people who lived as we did owned chainsaws and multiple sets of work gloves. Rural living required residents to put up with certain inconveniences. We got out of the car and quickly understood that our cursing wasn't going to dislodge the tree. Naturally, he was the one who handled the grunt work of chain sawing while I oversaw the operation and toted away the small branches and lopped-off foliage. It took a lot of sawing and toting. As we finally got all our luggage inside the house, we both rested and reflected. Well, he rested and I did most of the reflection.

Suddenly he got up from the cozy wing backed chair that seemed to comfort his aching back and looked at me smugly. "I think we should give us a break. Can you stand renting a place where it's warm for two whole months?"

I didn't have to utter a word, having finally learned in my whole struggling life that timing was everything.

✳✳✳

We bought a nice new house in Florida in the same year as the real estate taxes in Kerhonkson were doubled as a result of visionary county policies. Now we could enjoy hefty tax payments on two houses along with the joys of being snowbirds.

Chapter 12
THE DELICACY OF BALANCING AGING ISSUES WITH MALE AND FEMALE DIFFERENCES

Since I gave up my fight to bring my hormonal challenges up to the task of meeting my husband's hormonal toughness head on, I had succumbed to arguing on a lesser scale of anxiety. The devil always was in the details. The details I am referring to concerned my various aches and pains as a result of muscle tone starvation. I usually harnessed my lawyering skills to butter him up:

"Dear, I'm going to be sixty-five years old soon."

"That's too bad. Your appetite seems more like what Martina Navratilova ought to eat. But you could always take up tennis!"

"I can't do that at my age. Can't you accept that my finest qualities involve my willingness to put up with you?"

"So while you're putting up with me, I'll let you do the dishes and scrub the floors and you can do the inside of the windows and the refrigerator and dust the bookcases. Oh, I'll do the outside of the windows."

"My mother always had a maid for that stuff."

"Honey, I'm your maid and you're my maid and, together, we have it made."

"Joker. You're trying to change me."

"Actually, I gave up trying to change you. You're like the light bulb joke. It would take ten therapists to change you. Nine to listen to your whining and one to send you the bill for your entire life savings."

"Is that a commentary on my habits or on your attitude toward therapy?"

"No comment."

The honeymoon period had morphed into the realization period which had now morphed into the sarcasm period. Several instances come to mind, but our dinner table is one of those staging areas which seem to bring out the rising of blood pressures and the squaring off of territory. Here's a typical marital moment, and I'll refrain from referring to it as a squabble. I prefer the term "small talk." We're having a meal in our new house in South Florida....

✳✳✳

It's a weekday when we mutually agree to use up the leftover venison steak along with baked potatoes and a salad. After eight years of wedded bliss, his health nut philosophy and my desire to unravel my childhood mystique about nourishment no longer provided any surprises. When we married I did not entertain an intense probe of this facet of his personality—I walked right into the opposite of me quite blindly. His solutions to the problems of overweight and under-exercise had always been simple. My solutions to those two conditions continued to be complex. Now that medical expense began to assume a larger line item in our budget we had begun to have more frequent discussions on the subject.

He seldom begins the chat session until we sit down to a meal. He's a typical man of sparse rhetoric, since he has a Masters Degree in Economics. Economies of scale mean economies of words also. I can always tell when he's going through his wind-up, however—the importance of what he's about to say hangs heavy over the serving dishes reposing in the center of the kitchen table.

"Uh, dear," he'll remark, "Are you sure you want that entire potato? The big one covering your dinner plate? Maybe you'd like to split it?"

I look at him knowingly. He's on my case as gently as he can muster—like a medium-weight hammer. I get an exact picture of what he's thinking and why he's thinking it. He's much too smart to be direct with me, so he soft-pedals the fact that I announced yesterday that I was "watching my calorie count." I internalize the meaning of his comments quietly while my belly is murmuring and my taste buds are calling. I venture my answer.

"Dear, you know I don't split potatoes—I like to make a boat out of an oval-shaped thoroughly baked Idaho so I can fill it with fat-free margarine, sour cream lite and green onion sprinkles— you know, the way the restaurant chefs do when we go out. How can I make a boat out of a potato if the bow is separated from the stern?"

"Don't give me that cheap ship talk! I know you were a big deal sailor when you hung around with that older guy. I can't argue with you over food. Forget it! Eat your giant potato and be happy. I'm getting off the case!"

He has a way about him when he concludes his remarks. I see that he stops talking on a dime and turns his attention to his spinach. My thoughts wander around the room and end up in mid-air—like somebody just took my dessert away. The conversation becomes a one-way silent internal monologue—me to me.

"Why does he always deliver the punch line with so much punch?" I muse to myself, while I pick at my broccoli and side salad. "I can't keep up this back and forth volley where he's one of the players and also the referee." The one-sidedness of my situation sticks in my craw as my intricate thinking continues. "I'd feel a little bit better if he would at least gain a few pounds when we go to the Chinese Buffet. He always pigs out on those little square cakes that taste like they squeezed vanilla extract into a yellow sponge and covered it with Halloween frosting. Then he heaps on those midget-sized éclairs and the itty-bitty petit fours. He loads up his plate and goes back for more, while I have to do higher mathematics in order to decide if I can enjoy one scoop of ice milk—yaaah, it's not even real ice cream."

I turn to him and change the subject. "I'll put the dishes in the dishwasher while you scrub the grill, OK?" OK?.... "Where did he go now?" I discover I'm talking to the air in the room. He's already out on the patio, no doubt cleaning the grill, having left the table while I was still thinking up a comeback. At least I think he's on the patio—he could be outside talking to a neighbor or in the garage poking through his myriad plastic containers of assorted hardware. I'm still reacting to the fact that he had left the room so speedily. "How the hell did he get by me?" I was short on options and slowly returned to my place at the table, focusing on the amount of nourishment remaining in the potato and whether I could still enjoy it.

This food thing is his game to win and mine to lose. I usually surrender in the sixth inning because he's a man of normal weight and body shape while I have a roll around the equator that is my stomach where there should only be an indented waistline. God favored me with an amplitude of Middle Ages style pulchritude. I swallowed my pride and left half the potato.

While I struggle with the quest for eternal health and beauty, there are other incidents ruining my appetite and running my life. He has a habit of teasing me unmercifully about many things, but during mealtimes he cranks up his inventory of observations. I see that he watches everything I ingest and studies how I chew it. Sometimes my fork loses its aim and a bit of food falls off. He says, "What's the matter, can't find your mouth? Why don't you follow the sound of complaining—you'll catch up to it!" It's devastating when I consider the things I have to put up with: Negative self-image, poor eating habits, unattractive stomach roll, restaurant consternation and a sarcastic husband. I don't know how I do it.

I end each day realizing that he loves me and only wants me to take better care of myself. I also realize that I am wedded to my creature comforts. That's a tactful way I tell myself that I'm a teeny bit lazy about certain things. "Now how did I get this way?" I ask myself the most probing and deep-seated questions as I curl into fetal position when I'm ready to close my eyes. I can't get over my childhood upbringing. That's how I always resolve my issues—run to the past. He hates that. Well, he says he was never a child. I fall asleep and probably dream about my adolescence. Would that I could still have that tiny waistline again—the rather attractive hourglass figure I carried around before I had three kids. Oh well.

When I grew up Mother taught me that my husband would take care of me in every way, you know, like a princess—and don't start thinking what I think you're thinking—I'm no stereotype. I carry my own weight in this egalitarian world. It's just a little bit too much weight. He warned me that I would either have to stay home while he pursued his preferred activity, or join with him his way, and that way usually meant being undernourished. Mother didn't tell me everything either, just like the rabbi left out half of the obligations when we agreed to take on the whole megillah. And in front of witnesses, yet.

Chapter 13
GUESS WHAT'S COMING FOR DINNER? PART ONE

I was so innocently idealistic when I gave up my sophisticated suburban Chicago lifestyle to join forces with a Renaissance Man who lived in the sticks. It was easy. All I needed was to look deep into his greenish hazel eyes and feel the glow of promised contentment. Decisions flowed easily for me from feelings based on cloud-like and girlish fantasies.

Only now was I feeling certain gnawing inconsistencies in my well thought out plan. It had made sense for me to avoid a stress-filled single life based on grinding out a career as a solo attorney. But was I really prepared to pay the cost of giving up part of that dream? I kept asking myself challenging questions:

"Do I really miss my suburban Chicago town home with the peach carpeting and the Italianate dinette set? Shouldn't I have questioned my decision to move into these digs before negotiating a little? Why this place is in the upper reaches of nowhere! My friends back in Chicago can't even find it on the map."

I approach my nonapproachable husband to ask an untimely question. He's not approachable because he's not in a good mood today, and that's why any question I ask is untimely. I do it anyway because I'm at loose ends.

"Uh, honey, I'm thinking, uh, I will never live long enough to get to be a sitting judge in this county we live in."

"You interrupted my reading of Peanuts for that? What bug is up your butt now?"

"Oh, I'm sitting here and feeling out of sorts. I have needs and I need my human needs massaged."

"Later. I'll massage whatever you want. Right now I'm reading the paper."

"You don't understand. I'm not happy today. I need a pep talk."

"OK, here it is. Get off your behind and do something peppy. Is that sufficient? I'm not sending you flowers or buying you a be-jeweled watch. You can't change the date and time on your old watch. Oh, here's a good idea for what to do—go to the eye doctor and get your prescription for glasses updated. Then you can read the small markings on your watch."

I retreat to my little corner and realize that he can't wave a magic wand and make me into a Marilyn Monroe look alike. I don't want to be like her anyway. I just want to have fun. OK, I'll take Madonna or Cyndi Lauper.

He's back to the newspaper. I know he's reading the conser-vative political opinion piece because he keeps thumping at that column and vocalizing. "Yaaaahh! That's right! Bing! Just what I've been saying!"

"Who's he talking to? He says I talk to myself, but so does he. Is he waving his hand at some guru in the sky? It must be Buckley or that economist, what's his name, Laffer? All I know is, he's not thinking about me." Then I see that his mood has changed from bad to neutral. So I pick up those positive vibes. I see my mood is changing from lassitude to penetrating. I remember that I love him, and love is blind. Ouch, he's right about my eyeglasses. Am I set in my ways? Is that expression a code word for stubborn?

When a set-in-her-ways thrice-married woman like me meets up with a set-in-his-ways twice-married guy like him, who really gets more votes?"

I conclude my reverie with my answer to that philosophical query: "The winner is the one with the fewest gnawing inconsistencies."

That conclusion ends my session with me. There will be no check to pay out to any shrink this time. I'm a do-it-yourself mood swing analyst. Oh yes, and I need a new activity or hobby. Let's see....

✳✳✳

I found myself in the living room one dreary day in late October staring at the wood stove nestled below his stuff and my stuff. Our stuff seemed happy together. Neither the elk horns nor my now relocated modern art paintings seemed to complain. I was the one who inwardly fretted about accepting somebody else's hand-sewn butternut colored tweed drapes and chintz wallpaper. The best I could do was to characterize the decorating scheme as "eclectic" and accept that Archaeological Digest wasn't coming and that it was, indeed, a dreary day in October. We had married in the month of May, but even in Upstate New York, spring turns to summer and summer becomes autumn.

Then I noticed that my loving husband in the next room was humming along with his favorite taped bluegrass music and seemed in a rare mood. I saw him rummaging in his closet for his hunting gear.

"Dear, are you getting ready for deer season, dear?" I thought to myself, "too many deers or dears in that sentence."

"Of course, I have to make sure I have everything I need."

"Can I help?"

"With what? You want to polish my rifle? Here, I'll give it to you—the cleaning supplies are on my table."

"I know you're joking—I don't know the first thing about cleaning a rifle—I'm still not sure I even like guns."

"You knew when you married me that I hunted and shot and belonged to sporting clubs where all the members hunt and shoot."

"Of course, and you really looked cute in your camouflage outfit—remember how I ran breathlessly behind you when you took me along on your pheasant hunt—I nearly broke my big toe while I was trying to keep up with you."

"I forgot you hurt your big toe—is it better?"

"I'm not sure—I can't feel it any more."

"Oh, well you've got four others on that foot. Big deal."

"Again you're teasing me. Well, I can take it. Maybe I'll show you up and take up hunting myself!"

"I thought you said you didn't like guns!"

"Well, I didn't like moose stew either when you first talked about it, but now I like it—so what if I changed my mind!"

"You can't just go out and hunt—you have to learn how to shoot a rifle and take a hunter safety course and learn how to be careful—all these things are foreign to you—you're just a city girl, even if you're a lawyer, a mother and a pretty good cook."

"Thanks for the compliments. I called your buddy, Guy. He told me I could sign up for hunter safety and the course starts next week."

"OK, let's go try out my guns. I have to figure out which one you can handle—your ambition is stronger than your weak shoulders and you never exercise. From now on, you have to practice walking up that steep hill behind the house—I mean every day. You need to shed about fifteen pounds too."

"I'm glad you're so specific. What if I lose fourteen pounds? What if I lose seventeen pounds? What makes you such a wise-ass?"

"Let's see if you can leave off the second helpings of the entree tonight—we're having Sauerbraten."

"That dish you make with chunks of venison and the ginger snaps?"

"Yes, you said you liked it."

"I lied—I didn't like the ginger snap part."

"You didn't tell me you didn't like it."

"We were still in honeymoon mode. I loved all your meals! Everything tasted like ambrosia and nectar."

"And now?"

"I really didn't like the ginger snap part, but now I'm very interested in learning to shoot a rifle and hunt. Can't you appreciate one out of two?"

"We start tomorrow. We'll go to the range to practice after I take you upstairs to the gun safe and see if you can even put one on your shoulder."

Chapter 14

GUESS WHAT'S COMING FOR DINNER?—PART TWO

True to form, my hunting expert husband kept his promise to me and helped me learn how to use a rifle at various ranges. He praised me when I shot well, no matter how uncomfortable it seemed at the time. I learned how to do belly shots, sitting shots and even standing shots, although he warned me that standing shots were the most difficult and unlikely to produce a good result.

After going through all the proper moves, I entered the twelve-week hunter safety course and learned even more about strategies for shooting wild animals. Although I had to pass up that whole deer hunting season because I still wasn't licensed, I knew I was gearing up for the kill. If I could learn to be a lawyer after going through motherhood training, I could learn just about anything. The biggest problem was that men's hunting clothes didn't fit me—my husband's second set of camo pants felt funny around my waist and the jacket hung strangely around my thighs. I know that my thrifty mate didn't want to spend a lot of his own money outfitting me until I proved myself, so he didn't. I said I would manage. We practiced with every rifle he had and he realized he had to borrow a lever action model from a friend of his because it was the only one that seemed right for a short lady lawyer from Chicago. The following year I was completely ready and even my husband thought I could pull the trigger without shooting myself in the leg. I had dropped about fifteen pounds and, even though I still huffed and puffed going up the steep hill behind the house, I could do it without fainting. On the first legal morning, he pushed me out of bed at 3AM and told me to put on my gear. You don't argue with a man with all those weapons. He was careful that I had everything I needed which he had prepared the night before.

"You've got your orange vest on inside out," he commented, as I posed for him like a fashionista for a low-class magazine.

"Thanks."

I fixed the vest and got ready for the big morning. We left the house while the stars were still out and before breakfast. Since I hadn't had my fix of eggs and bagel, I felt needy. This hunting stuff required some habit-forming. It also required some undoing of prior habits. My worst problem was that I wouldn't be able to talk or breathe hard because the deer had such keen hearing and they would run away before I got into position. I would have to operate without an audience, which was tough for a ham like me. My positioning and patience went on for three mornings. Each mid-day I returned to the house empty-handed. On the third morning I had something positive to report:

"Honey, I saw three deer and one of them saw me and before I could get the gun out of my lap, they had bolted for the next door neighbor's acreage."

"That happens."

"Yes, but I spent all morning out there and it was cold and I was hungry. This hunting stuff aint all it's cracked up to be."

"Listen, you sheltered woman, you, how do you think Daniel Boone survived—did he get cold feet and go home to his kids and tell them, "Sorry, kids, no dinner tonite?""

"Well———"

"Yah, well! You wanted to hunt. If hunting were so easy, all the old ladies in the county would be doing it!"

"There are no old ladies in the county—hardly any old ladies live out here in the boonies!"

"What about Nancy down the road—she's old and she's lived here all her life! What about her?"

"Nancy doesn't have to hunt. She takes care of her mother— her mother's 103 years old."

"How do you think she survives out here? Do you think her husband, when he was alive, just went to the grocery store and came home with packaged frozen food? This is the country! Guys hunt and sometimes they sit for days and nothing happens!"

"OK, I get the idea. I'll try again tomorrow, but I'm not sitting out there where all the deer can see me—I'm going to find a place where I can see them and they can't see me!"

(Softly) "Honey, it's nothing personal, but they can smell you!"

"So I used the essence-free soap, like you taught me—I put on the female doe's urine perfume, like you taught me—I held my breath, like you taught me, and I did everything right. You'll see— tomorrow, don't take out the ribs from the freezer—I'm bringing dinner back from the woods."

"Dear, the carcass has to be aged for at least several days or it will be tough."

"What about my aging? I'm three weeks older in experience in only three days! Oh, never mind. But we'll have venison under glass next week and I'll figure out the recipe!"

"That'll be the day."

"Stop doing John Wayne."

"Go fold your laundry—I threw it on your side of the bed."

"What happened to your honeymoon voice?"

"Lovely woman, will you pleeeeeze fold your damned laundry?"

"I'm not living here next year."

"OK, I'll take note of that. Leave a message by the telephone—"Wife gone—shop for concubine. At least that will remind me."

"You suck."

With that exchange, I went to my private office space in the spare room, squeezed behind the desk and spat out $500 worth of billable tax work. Enough was enough and I would show up that wise guy I was hung up on. Daniel Boone indeed!

✳✳✳

Early the next morning I found just the right pine tree with just the right drooping branches with just the right embedded boulder by the bottom of the trunk where I could ensconce my behind and still lay the rifle across my knees. It was freezing and my gloves had iced up within twenty minutes. That's when I had to go pee. I stood up, carefully set the gun down and knew what I had to do. Suddenly, I heard a far-off shot. Somebody either nailed dinner or maybe wasted a perfectly good round. I hoped whoever it was wasn't peeking. I had difficulty getting my pants down and crouching like a pioneer woman would have done—the jacket was too long and I couldn't get the belt undone. At my age there was no time to waste. Soon it didn't matter any longer. Could deer tell the difference between a doe's pee and a city girl's pee? Maybe I would put that one on my list of questions for Mr. Know-It-All.

✳✳✳

I thought a half hour had ticked by, but I couldn't get to my watch because my left gloved hand was surrounded by icicles. A squirrel came along and squinted at me with a nut in its mouth. I felt hungry, but not that hungry. I knew people shot squirrels and made Brunswick stew out of them, but I probably wouldn't like Brunswick stew—especially if I had met the squirrel personally. Then I heard a suspicious rustle—what was going on? Ahead of me about three hundred feet down the slope by a small stream there came a procession of grayish brown animals—one by one. Yiiikes! What do I do now? Get the rifle! No, not that end—that's the business end! Take off the safety! Faster, you idiot—the deer don't have all day! Get one of them in my scope with the cross-hairs! Just like in the movies! Mommie! I can't do this, Mommie! That's Bambi out there! Well, I got this far, so,..... . suddenly I pulled the trigger and the recoil was brutal—just like in practice. Good thing I was a terrible shot. All the deer ran away anyway—like the fleet creatures as advertised. What's that? A straggler? What's that thing waving around down there? Wow! I got one! No, I don't believe it. This can't be happening to me! I was a nice girl from the city just this morning! Oh Lord, what do I do now!"

I remembered to wait fifteen minutes just in case the ending of a life wasn't quick. I remembered to say a brocha. Then I remembered that a deer wasn't Kosher, so why say a brocha? Then I wondered, didn't Abraham have to slay a sacrificial animal? So what's the big deal? There aren't any rabbis around. This is the country. I'm a wild woman. Nobody will believe this back home! Wait a minute! I am home! I live with this guy now! We got married! Plus, we don't keep Kosher! I guess I forgot all about that in my rush of adrenalin! Wow, my heart is pounding! Maybe I would have liked Brunswick stew after all. I guess I have to remove the critter's insides like I was taught. Oh, why was I born to grow up a rebellious Jewish princess like this? I could have stayed in Chicago playing mah jjonghh! I could have had fun with the girls and then gone out for barbequed ribs and a few glasses of wine. Life—I'm living life. I'd better say another brocha—this one's for me!"

***

I sat on the back door stoop and waited for my husband to return from his area of the woods. The ice on my glove had melted and my sleeves and gloves were drenched and my camo pants would need to go right into the wash—dirt, piss, deer blood, probably a few stray ants, and whatnot. I lingered for it was nearly eleven o'clock and I hadn't had breakfast. I thought it was ironic that I had just killed what would be our dinner for a whole week and I didn't even get a slice of rye bread that morning. Then he came down the hill, gun slung along his back, humming a little tune, maybe happy to see me—maybe not. He called out: "Hey, I'm going to take you out to lunch. We can go to the diner down the road! Isn't that nice of me?"

"Whoa, boy, whoa, boy. Not so fast. This is Annie Oakley you're addressing."

"Yeah, Annie, I'm sorry, I know you tried hard and I'm proud of you. Let me get washed up and you should change clothes." He had gotten closer to me. "You really did put on that doe urine, didn't you?"

"That's not all from the doe, Buster—I'm a real woods woman now, and I'm going to need your assistance for the next hour or so."

"How so?"

"I can't drag that cotton-pickin' buck all the way here without your handle and stuff—you gave me a little twig to work with and I got a big fucker!"

"You? You got a deer?"

"Who do you think you're married to? Your Aunt Goldie? You taught me what to do and I did it. Let's go get it."

My husband's face got purple with envy, and then he realized that he had been the brains behind the slaughter. He broke out into the cutest grin I'd seen on him since that day his stock portfolio took a spike. He realized that I wasn't such a loser after all. We embraced, while he turned his nose away.

"Wait till the boys at the gun club find out," he muttered, just loud enough for me to hear. "My wife got a buck—how many points did it have? What, six? Oh man, my wife got a six-pointer and I got shit. They're going to razz me from now to Christmas."

We went back up the hill and brought our kill down to the shed. I noticed he talked about it as "our" kill, not "my" kill. When it served him, we shared. We never did get to the diner for lunch. I had to content myself with leftover moose stew. But the following Wednesday evening we went to the gun club dinner and the guys toasted me and roasted me. I was voted the Queen for the meal. The Queen got to collect the dishes at the end of dinner for sixty-five hungry red-necked loud-mouthed hicks. What a motley group! Suddenly, I loved every one of them and I felt happy. I guess I was home. As we left the club that evening after a fine meal, I waved goodbye to all the animal mounts hung on the walls with the huge blank eyes staring at each other. They didn't get to enjoy dinner that night—they had months ago been dinner. I tried to whistle an old country song, but then I remembered that I didn't know how to whistle, so I went home exhausted with my sweet husband, who was also exhausted, and we snored the night away.

Chapter 15
LIFESTYLE CHANGES IN THE WIND

I figured that my third husband and I would be traveling quite a bit because his unwritten resume read like a description of the career of a daring photojournalist. He and his first wife had lived in Mexico and Greece for months at a time and had traveled extensively throughout Europe and the Caribbean. I had driven an unbelievable number of miles to and from the residences of my children in the Chicago area and later added to my mileage total when I began to embark on a series of USA auto trips to escape the residences of my children.

Before our nuptials, I asked him to give me a straight answer to my penetrating question:

"Honey, when you leave the United States with your camera equipment and all, do you take chances with your safety? Like go to Third World places where they could pick you up for loitering with intent to photograph?"

"Naah, I'm a coward."

"Why do you say you're a coward?"

"I haven't gone to Israel and I'm Jewish."

"OK, you brought it up—why haven't you gone to Israel?"

"Because nothing ruins a vacation more than being blown up on a bus ride."

"Oh my, that's a pretty extreme view, don't you think?"

"Yup."

"Yup? What kind of word is that? Did you veg out on too many cowboy movies? Did your living in this tree frog-infested zone that your best friend characterizes as Tobacco Road turn your head? You're a nice Jewish boy from Chicago, just like I'm a nice Jewish girl from there—where does this macho streak in you come from?"

"I dunno. Stop talking about it. You're a real nag. However, I love you anyway."

"That's a good thing, that you love me. Does your being influenced by your rural, uh, redneck, friends have anything to do with your engagement present to me?"

"Maybe. I guess you're referring to my little joke."

He was referring to the small package he had sent me in the mail while I was preparing for our wedding. Since the only ring I was to be given was a gold wedding band, he had decided to bestow some tangible symbol of his love and fidelity on me so that I could show my friends and my family, all of whom I would soon be abandoning, what my latest husband thought would make an appropriate substitute for a two-carat marquee. I called him as soon as I opened his unexpected present.

"Honey," I just got this strange object with your letter. Is this supposed to be a funny joke?"

"Don't you like it?"

"It" was a brown knobby thing attached to a fastener which came on a card with the descriptive wording: "Moose Turd Pin."

"I know what a turd is—I'm not a purist that never peeks—but why a moose one?"

"That's all they had that looked good. I didn't think you'd like the one that read "Bear Scat Brooch.""

"OK, but if I decide to wear it, I'm not sure what outfit will go with it."

"I'll buy you a red necked lady's outfit from Cabela's after you vow you'll never leave me."

"Here's my vow: I promise I'll never leave you and I promise that I'll wear this pin only to your gun club events or similar occasions. But I have to warn you: I only do diamonds at my weddings."

"I realize you've had multiple experiences, honey, and all my friends know I'm taking a big chance. If you continue with your spendthrift ways, we won't be able to afford trips to places like Peru or Australia or Waterford County in Ireland, where they have that beautiful glass."

"You win."

"OK. You don't have to send me a thankyou note for the pin."

"I really adore you."

"How could you help it?"

That conversation proved to be prophetic. A year or two later, as I accustomed myself to poring over my new subscription to Outdoor Life after allowing my subscription to Bazaar to lapse, I tried to reconstruct how it all happened. I remembered that afternoon during the engagement period when I had hurried to an antique and jewelry show to sell some of my baubles and had come home with a thousand dollars. I can still feel the remnants of the afterglow I basked in as I savored my newfound streak of thrift. I think I fingered those ten crisp one hundred dollar bills over and over until I realized that the walnut armoire in my bedroom now had some empty slots. I had made a dent in my need to be a symbol of upper class extravagance, but my actions had not quite caught up to my inner desires. I used the money to pay off part of one of my credit cards. That was a good day, financially speaking. But to be really sincere, I have to admit that I continued to pine after one of the gold chains that went with absolutely everything.

Chapter 16
HOLIDAY CHEER IN A LONG BOX

After our wedding and our adjustment to each other's michigas[5] in several important ways, the traveling and other elective activities began in earnest. I had a semi-retired husband and I had a home office portable computer-based tax practice, which gave us lots of free time to wander about the hemisphere. However, he always had to have a purpose for his travel other than ogling another country and then sending postcards to the daughter and a few buddies. A trip required either relaxation at a warm and tropical island getaway, or it had to be about hunting and/or photography. And that's really how the following saga began, quite soon after I had begun to exhibit my shooting skills.

After the six-pointer had been skinned, dressed, butchered and served up in a variety of tasty ways, I prepared for the holiday season, which I used to think of as Hanukah. Now we just spoke of it as Christmas for Jewish people, and we decided to exchange presents on the morning of the 25th of December. Neither of us even looked at the calendar to see the dates of actual Hanukah, but I inadvertently learned of them from one of my orthodox clients. Hanukah had passed me by a week earlier.

The dawn of the Christian savior's birth brought us downstairs to unwrap the gifts. My stepdaughter and her boyfriend attended, as well as the over-the-hill hunting dog, who remained awake for the first fifteen minutes of the event. That pooch normally slept 23 hours a day. It isn't important for me to mention any of the gifts exchanged that morning except the big one for me, which came in a box shaped like it might contain a large umbrella. I lifted the box and it was too heavy for even the sturdiest of bumbershoots. That's when I knew who I really was: Mrs. Sharpshooter. My new rifle was a bolt action gem by Winchester, Model 70, an inspired adaptation by the venerable manufacturer expressly for accuracy and ease of use. When I realized what my thrifty mate had paid for this gun, I sensed that a serious emotional conflict might be coming on. Never in a million years would I have guessed that one day the love of my life would demonstrate his devotion in this manner. The three of them looked at me, anticipating some sort of interesting reaction. Even the dog woke up. I had to speak without saying something ridiculous.

"Honey, you wouldn't have put your money on the line for me unless you thought I deserved it—isn't that so?"

"I don't know what I thought. If you're serious about hunting, you need the proper gun."

"Are you sure that this isn't a model made for weak men and middle-aged ladies?"

"It's a fine gun. I bought it for you because you did well and worked hard."

"Well, I'm having a hard time dealing with this." I knew I was on the edge of tears and that nobody in the room would understand why someone with such steely determination as I would suddenly exhibit childish behavior. "I have to excuse myself, folks," I explained, as I ran out of the room to grab some tissues from the bathroom. Although I tried to tough it out, I had lost all control. Shutting the bathroom door, I sat on the toilet lid and let the sobbing begin.

After a few minutes I heard a knock on the door and my husband's voice called out: "Are you mad at me because I said something nice?"

"I'm not mad at you. I'm emotional because this is the best present I've gotten in my whole life!"

"Oh, well can you open the door, then?"

I opened the door and he was standing there, absolutely dumbfounded. He obviously didn't know what to make of the whole scene, so I kissed him. That seemed to help.

"Thank you, thank you," I whispered, composing myself.

"Does this mean you're happy? I got confused there for awhile."

"Haven't I explained to you before that sometimes tears mean great joy?"

"Well, how will I know when you're sad? Will you be laughing?"

"No. And don't try to understand it. Let's go back to the living room. I want to see what's in the little package."

"Oh, I forgot. Well, it goes with the gun."

"Ammo?"

"No, I'll take care of that. Just open the other gift."

So I unwrapped the small box and out came a brand new watch. I held it up for everyone to observe.

"It's totally waterproof, you see," he explained. "It's good for all kinds of weather. When you're out hunting, you might get caught in a storm."

Somehow I managed to keep my cool.

The next day I woke up feeling exhilarated about my new present. Not only was it the very first firearm that was all mine—it was a gun I could show off to at least two other people I knew, while all the rest of my friends would assume I had gone over the edge. My deer conquest had not only toyed with my mind—it had revealed something about my nature. How could I pretend now that I wasn't a gunslinger at the gut level, now out of the closet? Had I come this far from being a balabuste?[6] These were heady concerns.

While still in my pajamas I had to look at my present one more time. My husband had put it in the safe, but I prodded him to take it out so I could gaze at it fondly and take in the new awesome feeling of gun ownership. I slid my hands across the barrel and smiled rather coyly. I had to say the right kind of words of appreciation to my darling.

"It's sooooo cute!"

"Sure it is. That six-pointer you nailed last month was the most expensive deer we ever ate."

"I'll take very good care of this lovely rifle."

"That'll be the day."

"No, I'll clean it after every excursion and everything."

"Can I put that on tape?"

"Don't you trust me?"

"To clean your rifle every time required? No."

"I want to go on a hunt other than in our back yard."

Did I mention that our back yard was twenty-one and one-half acres of pristine unlogged natural forest? If I'm repeating myself, well, so sue me—I'm redundant and I'm also the lawyer. But I still had to remember that every time I wandered back there, every tree, every rock, every weed, looked similar. Landmarks were good, but how could I orient myself when the sun was hidden, the fallen down limbs were everywhere and every maple or oak looked alike? Each time I decided to explore the far reaches of our portion of the county, I was forced to bring a compass. My husband's constant admonition was drilled into my head:

"If you go out in the woods and forget your gun, with a compass you can always find your way back home and get it. If you forget your compass, well, you know that story about Davy Crockett, don't you?"

"What?"

"I told you. One day when Mr. Crockett hadn't been seen for about sixty hours by his concerned family, a search party went out in the woods to look for him. They found the fellow lying against a tree stump looking messy, dehydrated and badly insect-bitten. "What happened, Davy?" his friend inquired. "Did you get lost here in the woods?" Davy rose to his full height despite his ordeal and answered vigorously: "Of course not—I've never gotten lost in the woods!"

Then he added sheepishly, "However, I did become somewhat confused for about four days."

"You told me that story before—twice before, I think."

"You don't listen."

"I heard every word."

"Then why can't you learn to use the compass like I taught you?"

"I keep forgetting why there are two needles."

"You're a lawyer—how do you keep track of the laws for your clients?"

"That's different. I have books to refer to. When I'm out in the woods I don't have books."

"You'd better take some hardtack, jerky and toilet paper next time you go."

"I can shoot, you know."

"Yes, that's what I'm afraid of."

So we continued with our pact of continued reprimanding of me for my wayward habits. It didn't stop us from planning the real hunting excursion—the trip of my dreams—CARIBOU HUNTING. We were to go to a part of Quebec far away from civilization, where the land was untamed and the weather was challenging.

Now I understood why I got the waterproof watch.

Chapter 17
PRELUDE TO AN ARCTIC EXPERIENCE

I knew very little about caribou other than the information I got from National Geographic. Then, two years into our marriage, we took a trip to Alaska, where we saw the signs that indicated the crossing point of the largest herd. The animals actually walked under the oil pipeline, which had been raised to a height to accommodate their overland route. I will never forget that pipeline because I was prompted to touch it. It was warm and the permafrost was cold. I'm so happy I got to see for myself all those sights that I used to read about in magazines.

We tromped all over the largest state in the U.S.A. and even took a plane from Fairbanks to Kotzebue—a small remote village north of the Arctic Circle. My most vivid memory of that place was the size of the mosquitoes. Big grasslands drew hordes of big bugs. Someone joked that the mosquito was the national bird of Alaska. I got to see places I had never dreamed of seeing. The natives were very clever at getting us tourists interested in their hobbies and business ventures. We were treated to a special presentation of Inuit women creating elaborate winter parkas made from animal skins. I was tempted to buy one and bring it home with me until my husband got wind of the price. We had to get back on the plane and allow the Kotzebue economy to muddle along without my help.

I suppose that Alaskan trip whetted my appetite for the far North. Now I knew for myself that the nature editors hadn't lied. Even in the summer months, the northernmost reaches of Alaska were only superficially temperate with the tillable soil area limited. Permafrost was real. I also realized that going to the far North beyond civilization would require a sturdy presence on my part. All I had to do now was prove that I could be a little bit sturdier than I looked. I expanded my exercise routine and used the gym in Kingston more frequently. The upcoming hunt in Northern Quebec was about to begin. Although I read the brochures over and over, the descriptions sounded a bit too good to be true. I asked a couple of simple questions of my experienced spouse:

"I've looked at the photos of all your hunting trips. Everybody seems smiling and happy, but isn't it all about male bonding?

"No, of course not. It's about successful hunting."

"Do you think I can hack it, really?"

"Sure you can. You'll do fine. You'll be one of the guys."

Chapter 18

FEELING LOST IN THE TUNDRA WITHOUT A SHRINK IN SIGHT— PART ONE

My new opportunity to prove I could really be "one of the guys" was a welcome autumn vacation from what had become the usual routine at home—scrubbing the algae-filled swimming pool, which often became a tadpole terrarium, and cleaning out the goat shed. The goats were long gone, but their hardened leavings were not. Spiders and other creatures now inhabited that area, which was the only place I had available to store garden tools. I figured that a camping experience and an opportunity to knock off a couple of caribou cows would be more fun than dodging insects and things that seemed to land on my hairdo—probably because they were attracted to my scented spray net.

I asked as few detailed questions as possible because I knew I would chicken out if I knew too much. "Where is this hunting camp, honey?"

"Look on the map."

"I did. It was off the charts."

"Well, it's uninhabited—maybe Rand McNally didn't bother to ink in the thousands of little lakes and gullies up there. Don't worry—the outfitters know what they're doing."

"I'm not worried about the outfitters—I'm worried about me."

"Don't be concerned—eventually they'd find your body and give you a decent burial—at least what was left of you after the predators had at it. You'll be fine."

"I like how you protect me."

"It's not fair—you never worry about protecting me!"

"Do we have to go through this all over again? When you fell off that stepstool onto the blacktopped driveway and ruined your shoulder, I tried to catch you!"

"That's not what I'm talking about. I'm talking about the time you pointed the rifle in the wrong direction while you were learning how to work the safety."

"Oh. Well, it didn't go off."

"Not then."

"I love you."

"You're the beneficiary on my life insurance."

"I'm not that kind of person."

"I'm teasing you."

"I hate when you do that. I get roped in every time."

"That's part of your charm."

✱✱✱

So we packed our stuff and drove up to Montreal to catch the first of two airplanes—a big commercial plane. I had been informed that the second leg of the journey would be made in a small cramped plane. That's when I visualized my worst fears— that of death by abandonment in the Wild North. Then I realized that I could get my fifteen minutes of fame posthumously. My descendants could tell tales about me and how some rugged explorers found my body in the frozen permafrost the way they stumbled onto the remains of the Vikings. It was of some comfort.

We flew to a place about a thousand miles north of Montreal where the plane began to circle—I hoped for a soft landing. We circled until I got dizzy, but I was able to peer out a window. There was some hint of habitation in the distance, and as we got closer, I was able to discern rows of dead seals along a shore. I thought, "Somebody down there must own some really large frying pans." I was told we were about to land in a town named Kuujjuuak. That's a bunch of u's and a couple of j's surrounded by k's. They don't call the Kuujjuuak natives Eskimos any longer—they too were referred to as Inuit, like the Alaskans. But igloos were still igloos, thank goodness. I had always wanted to see a real igloo close up. However, it wasn't to be. In Kuujjuuak, I was told that the native peoples lived in Canadian subsidized housing and survived on basic foodstuffs that got flown in and were available in a large commissary. The Inuits provided their own meat by hunting and fishing. But that's not where our outfitters took people like us rugged hunting types. Kuujjuuak was too civilized. Really? I looked for edible plants while we dilly-dallied around the airport, but didn't see anything green growing. I asked what did grow there and was told the vegetation was mainly black spruce and lichens.

"Lichens?" I remembered that term from my botany course. "Who or what eats lichens?"

I was told that the members of the deer family, including caribou, thrive on the stuff. I figured it was time to quiz my husband about the details of our lodging, since Kuujjuuak was only a pit stop and a place to get a plane that could land on water. What if they served lichens at the camp where we were headed? Yiikes.

"Sweetie, honey, uh, what kind of a lodge are we staying at?"

"You asked me that before. Remember I told you that it was a bit on the rough side? Didn't I show you those photos of the time I went to that camp in Newfoundland?"

"Yes, you did, dear. You were in a room with two other guys like a motel room."

"Well, don't you remember that I told you that we are going way up North where they have to put up makeshift shelters?"

"You mean, like, a tent?"

"Sort of."

"Well, will they have a tent for just you and me?"

"I'm not really sure. Oh, now I recall it might be nine guys and you and me."

"No other. . ladies?"

"Hey, you can handle it! You're a proven outdoorswoman how! Even the gals around here can't shoot worth a darn. Oh, now that I think of it, I did see one blonde woman a couple of years ago on a moose hunt in Newfoundland. You wouldn't have been able to hunt there because the walking is too difficult. But she was gorgeous and she had great, I mean, strong, legs. Also, she was one hell of a shot."

"So what's wrong with Northern Quebec where we're going? Why can't a lady hunter besides me go there?"

"Dunno. They just don't."

"I think I'm staying put here where it's still above freezing."

"OK, I'll ask another woman—I'll find somebody."

"I'm coming—I'm teasing."

We left the small terminal at Kuujjuuak and said good-bye to the Inuit attendants working the counter. Now we boarded a very small plane with pontoons and about twenty passengers, nineteen men and me. However, the pilot was a woman who resembled my idea of what Amelia Earhart would have looked like if her old photographs had been less flattering. She was very helpful and I had a snapshot of the two of us taken before the flight took off. At least my kids would have a memento. As the plane's engines revved up, I caught sight of the Kuujjuuak terminal and realized that the word "terminal" was a good word. We were now about to depart from the North end of civilization. I just couldn't wait to meet my nine other roommates.

❊❊❊

The plane bucked and rolled a lot and I nearly fell into the lap of a pretty good-looking fellow, but my seat belt held. I could feel us descending and poked my head as close to his window as possible, despite all the gear stacked every which way. I figured the FAA hadn't sanctioned this particular flight. I didn't want to know anything more about how these private planes operated. From my seat companion's window I eyeballed the terrain below us and couldn't see anything but water.

I asked my seat buddy, "Where is the land?"

"Not much of that," he replied.

"Hell, we're almost on the water! We're not landing here, are we?"

We landed here.

Amazingly, the plane's able woman pilot had known her way around and we touched down on a strip of gravelly grassy surface that felt somewhat solid. There was no tarmac at all—just a runway that looked like it was as long as it needed to be without an inch to spare. Still, I felt relieved to be on the ground. There, in the distance, I could see smoke coming out of a structure. I hoped it was the kind of smoke that was from cooking and not from something burning down. We were ushered, with our gear being handled by two guys on ATV's, into a makeshift enclosure that bore the odor of grease. I was told it was our dining room. We had a meeting of the camp goers and the outfitters inside that room, sort of a mess hall, where I gazed at the shelves of canned food while trying to listen to the rules of the hunt. I could multi-task fairly well, but I was really worried about the meals, because I had been on a fairly successful high fiber diet. I wondered if they had brought broccoli.

"Dear, I'm looking at all the food that they have on those shelves, but I can't see what's in the huge fridge thing. Like where are the salad ingredients?"

"No fresh veggies here. It's just too hard to fly them in."

"Well, uh, how will I stay, uh, regular?"

"I told you and you didn't listen. I brought lots of fiber pills."

"But that's not enough."

"Oh, I know. I didn't want to upset you. I always get constipated when I go to hunting camp. You'll get over it, unless, of course, you die out here."

"Will I dream?"

"Lady hunters usually survive. Men have a way of being protective, even at 62° North latitude. They'll take care of you. Just take the fiber pills."

"I'll gain weight—I know they have high calorie meals because I can see all the deep frying equipment from where I'm sitting."

"You'll do a lot of walking. Trust me."

"I still have to fit inside my camo outfit—we didn't buy this new outfit in a roomy size, you know."

"You don't want ill-fitting clothes. As you walk the many miles out to the hunting site, you'll actually sweat. You took your down vest and several sweaters, so you'll be shedding layers of clothes by the time we've gone about ten miles."

"Are you going to walk slower for me?"

"It's very hard for me to slow down. Remember I told you that you had to keep up? That's why I drummed into you how to use the compass!"

"What compass?"

"Aha! I outsmarted you. I took two extra compasses because I know about your careless habits. Still, I'm not ready to lose you to the ravages of the North. I still like your cooking and you're getting better at cleaning the swimming pool. When I get you home, I want you to come up with a great caribou meat recipe. That's the reason I want you to live."

"Good. I'm feeling comforted. I guess we're not going to sleep together on this week away from all things civilized."

"No, you'll be in your sleeping bag and I'll be in mine, and the other nine guys will each be in theirs."

"Where will I change from my clothes to my pj's?"

"Inside the sleeping bag."

"It sounds kind of hard to do."

"Not so hard—just don't lose your brassiere, because the guys will razz you if they find it."

"I'm going to journalize all this, you know."

"That's OK, just don't get lost. Oh, at night we'll be able to see the Northern Lights."

"I hope I can stay up to see them."

"You'll have to, because I know your habits. You always have to pee in the middle of the night and there are no outhouses here."

"You mean…"

"Yes, you'll go way back of the tent and do your stuff."

"What about my behind? I'll freeze it!"

"You'll be quick about it then."

"Gee, I've never even thought about seeing the Northern Lights, much less pee while I'm gazing at them."

"It'll be a first for you then. You might even enjoy it."

Our tent was the largest one in the camp. As soon as we entered, five guys inside saw me right off and immediately ceased swearing. One scrambled into his slacks before I got too good a look at his Ralph Lauren jockey shorts.

"Oh, hi," I said as I waved," "Don't worry about me—I've seen cute jockey shorts before. Plus I can listen to filthy jokes if you know some good ones."

"Oh, hi, miss, we knew you were arriving, but we thought they would put you up at the women's dorm."

"There is no women's dorm."

"Really? They used to have one."

"That was before they lowered the prices a bit. Now they keep us all cozy together. My husband here—he told me that the money they save gives us better food and more guides. I'm used to being with men." I nearly revealed that I had been married a few times, but then I decided that it was too soon to become intimate. Instead I blurted out: "It's OK for you guys to talk freely, since I'm a married woman!"

"Nice to meet you. I'm married too, but she doesn't like hunting."

"I'm not surprised. I'm out to prove something. She probably doesn't need to."

"We've been married for thirty years."

"That's what I meant."

"You mean you're newlyweds?"

"Not exactly. We've made it for five years in a row and I think I passed the test."

"You seem like a nice woman, so I'll tell you straight out—THIS IS THE TEST!"

"I knew that."

My husband was always initially quiet with new people. He had been nervously observing my friendly conversation with one of the men with whom we would be living for a week. One of us always had to be the first one to break the ice of casual conversation and that one was usually me. I glanced at him to assure myself that he wasn't showing signs of being sorry that I had come along. He seemed fairly comfortable—at least I hadn't embarrassed him yet. It was too soon to expect him to break out into a smile, but at least he spoke to me before turning his attention to more important things, like the items he had to unpack. I watched him while he performed like a veteran camper. Then he turned his head to say something that would help me emotionally.

"See what wonderful experiences you're having? When we get back home you can phone your kids and wow them. Maybe your son will have a better job by then."

"Don't get your hopes up."

"Don't you think about your kids while you're up here?"

"Actually, most of my thinking involves my behind."

"Well get off it—unpack please. Do I have to be your wet nurse?"

"I'll ignore the implications in that statement. But seriously, do I have any time at all to relax today?"

"No. This isn't a spa. Let's get to the mess hall for lunch. Get your gear together. We're burning daylight."

Chapter 19

FEELING LOST IN THE TUNDRA WITHOUT A SHRINK IN SIGHT— PART TWO

The prospect of eating a hunting camp meal was beginning to feel like heaven. There was a great deal of food. I lunched on home-made meatloaf, mashed potatoes, canned peas, canned applesauce, three cups of coffee, a slice of chocolate cake and, just to be on the safe side, only one oatmeal cookie. I hadn't counted up the calories, but I felt somewhat secure that my upcoming hike of about twenty miles, ten going and ten returning, would use up at least 500 calories. Of course, I had no idea what I was getting into.

Predictably, my husband finished eating first and, noticing my slower pace, spoke sharply to me:

"We haven't got all day—go get your gun ready and your vest and your backpack and lace up those long boots we bought you— hurry up your ass!"

"Is this the way you're going to talk to me from now on?"

"No, I'm being sweet now. Wait a little bit. This is hunting camp—not ladies' tea. You'll see. And use your damned compass like I showed you!"

I wondered—why was he acting so strict and bossy all of a sudden? Then I realized that he was under some tension regarding his own performance, as well as having to worry about me. I stopped trying to judge him and switched my attention to the matter of handling my gear the way we had practiced. I had already forgotten how to use the compass, so again he helped me set the appropriate needle in the direction of camp. We began our first trek to the area where the guides had seen some of the herd. A strong wind blew in my face as I stared at the trail ahead. The landscape was unbelievable. Right off the bat, I realized that we were at a place where no man had gone before, except for the few ATV's and an unknown number of prior hunters. I really did feel like I was living in a scene right out of Star Trek. The footsteps of others before us were now encrusted in the nearly frozen mud. They must have been big fellows—their boot sizes seemed extremely large.

We passed a small forest of dwarf black spruce trees surrounded by low-bush blueberries and red currant-like fruit on plants that dotted the ground. Everything underfoot consisted either of soft mud puddles or small patches of wild grass. I was quick to learn that if I stepped on one of the patches incorrectly, my boot would sink about a foot into muddy water and I could injure an ankle. Yards ahead of us, perched on relatively flat terrain, were the most massive boulders I had ever seen. I learned months later that they were probably referred to as "erratics," but at the time the only words I had available to describe them were "those giant rocks." That reference didn't do them justice, but I was with a bunch of hunters and their guides, with nary a geologist in the entire camp. The presence of the boulders gave the surrounding area a surreal look—as though we had landed on another planet. These giant formations, eroded over the years into rounded orbs, were quite spectacular. They were composed of granite, quartzlike chunks, shale-like pieces and some other materials that I could not identify. Their stark presence served to remind me that **I** was the intruder and that **they** had been there for aeons. Later on I was told that nobody knew exactly how long they had been there.

I wished that I could have resurrected my knowledge of rocks and minerals, but now all I could think about was that I wished these formations had been better shaped to provide some shelter from the wind.

My husband was walking beside me for a half mile or so, but then turned to me. "Will you be OK if I go at my own speed?"

"Of course, dear. You said this wasn't Ladies Tea. I'm ready to kill something. If I wasn't, then why am I shlepping this rifle?" He seemed satisfied that I wasn't going to complain any more than usual and began hurrying his pace, while I hurried my pace. Our respective paces differed, like, a lot.

The further we hiked the more relentless the wind seemed. I shouted at the quick-moving air: "Damn you—where do you get off blowing like this?" It really helped my situation. I began to get hoarse and then I had something new to complain about in addition to my cold face. My thoughts were self-serving, as usual, and my ongoing struggle to rid myself of negative grumblings continued. I began to rail against the forces of nature, as though ranting aloud would decrease my discomfort. "Say, God, why didn't you make those boulders more accommodating? You could have had some little caves in there, or at least somewhere around here where I could have warmed up a bit!" I seemed to lose all inhibition about expressing my feelings loudly, as I realized that neither the cold wind nor the group ahead of me could hear anything I said. They seemed focused on finding animals to kill, while I was focused on the injustice of the fact that neither man nor nature was going to pay homage to a nice lady from a temperate climate.

The rattling of the earmuffs of my orange hunter hat only got worse as the wind velocity increased. Doubts about whether I could do this hike at all seemed to haunt me. Should I have turned back and humiliated myself by copping out? I gave myself advice at every step. "I can't turn around now—my hunting activities would be toast! What would my husband, the provider of the funds for this trip, say to me and how would he feel? He would stew in his juice for the remainder of our stay." I couldn't begin to tally up the unpleasant consequences.

As I pressed on, because it was the only logical thing to do, I kept up my audible chatter to cushion my growing sense of despair. I was freezing and wished I had dressed with more layers. Suddenly I realized I was being a poor sport and began to goad myself into thinking positively. "How about a song?" I started humming 'Ole Man River.' "Now why did I pick that one?" I could have picked out 'Against the Wind', or 'Baby It's Cold Outside'—something that made more sense! Then I thought better of it. That old Cole Porter ballad had the power to help me elevate my attitude— in a few yards my mindset had progressed from self-pity to a little smidgeon of courage.

I pretended I was in a war and that after I had fulfilled my mission I was going to get a medal. That seemed to toughen me up. What if I were in the Army and I could get kicked out of boot camp for being soft? I kept on tromping through the swampy stuff, because I had no honorable way out.

My husband, seemingly in his element with three other guys, plus two guides, was now about three hundred feet ahead of me and I could see the distance between us increasing. He did look back occasionally to see if I was keeping up and once he even dropped back to help me as I waded through a foot of muddy gook. He said something kind: "You're doing OK—just try to keep up—if you get too far behind—follow that trail where the ATV tracks are. Also, you're pretty good at observing landmarks—you will probably recognize each of these giant rocks."

"Rocks? You call them rocks? That one over there is the size of Toledo! And there ahead of us? That one's Cleveland! I get it.

You know you're going to disappear as you hang out with the guys. Don't worry about me—I'm just trudging along and singing."

"How can you sing in this wind?"

"It's extremely hard. I'm getting quite hoarse. But it makes me forget about my feet."

"You'll need your feet. You only have about six and one-half miles to go."

"I really needed that statistic. Can't you humor a person?"

"Do you want a funny joke now?"

"Go 'way. I'm extremely busy. Plus, I can't waste any energy talking. Only six and one-half miles to go. Gee." Then I had a great idea of what to say before he disappeared ahead. "Did anybody ever tell you that you talk too much?"

The most difficult part of the hike to the destination that afternoon was an enormous area of low-lying patches of wild grass and klutzy shrubs that were so far apart, growing out of the gooky water, that I had to stretch my poor legs plus maintain my balance to keep from rolling an ankle. That slowed me up considerably, and this went on for what seemed like a long half hour and then I had to scramble up a steep muddy hill where I searched for handholds and hung onto those wonderful blueberry plants for dear life. When I got to the top I saw the guys waiting for me. One guide had been assigned to my husband and me, since we were the twosome that required special handling. He took us off in one direction, while the other guide took the other guys in another. We were atop a hill at an interesting vantage point, and I felt I could see forever into the distance—at least one one-hundredth of the way back to Kuujjuaak. The guide had decided to do one of us at a time and I was first. He motioned for me to hunch down. I liked that—anything to get off my feet.

"OK, now you get down behind the weeds where I tell you and get your rifle in position. I think we're going to get lucky."

"Does lucky mean there's a caribou coming?"

"Lucky means I can hear something in the distance. Stop talking."

I whispered, "I understand." I didn't understand anything except that I was being shushed and primed for some sort of confrontation. I saw the guide point silently to an area about two hundred yards from where I was sitting. Sure enough, there was something moving out there. My heart began to pound. I looked at the guide and he was nodding. We had gotten lucky very quickly. The animal soon showed itself and stood up. It was a target. I knew this because the guide whispered, "Shoot, damn it—she's not going to wait around for you!" I shot twice and that was that. The guide said in a normal voice: "Good girl—you're a good shot. She's finished. Just stay here and I'll get your husband going."

It was good to be a "girl" again instead of a crab. I stayed there and watched everything there was to watch. I could no longer see my victim, but I knew it wasn't going anywhere. I could hear three shots nearby. Then the two of them found me crouching and hugging my rifle and told me we had each gotten the first of our quota. We were allotted two each. The guide told me to go a little bit down a slope and then stop. I did what I was told. He pointed again and I saw two animals—now I knew they were caribou cows. This time I knew what to do without coaching. "Bang!" I nailed one of them and then looked at the guide. We both saw the other cow take off in a heartbeat. The guide seemed satisfied that I was a killer. He said to me: "We have to start walking now to go to where your husband can get his second animal. You can stay here or follow us. If you stay here, I'll come back for you."

"I'm not staying here all alone. I'll follow you guys."

I got up and shouldered my gun and thought about a snack. The cook, a fat Newfoundland woman, had packed two sandwiches of ham and cheese on white bread for me. I had no intention of eating anything on white bread, especially before the big evening meal, but in this wilderness, well, maybe I'd change my mind. The two guys walked fairly rapidly and I couldn't keep up with them. It was not a big surprise. They disappeared over a hill and I realized that I might have to use the compass after all. The wind, which had lessened a bit during my stint at killing, now came up again fiercely and the temperature seemed about thirty-five degrees. Calling out was useless—the distances and wind conditions were too challenging. I kept walking where I thought they had headed, following what I prayed was their foot trail.

I came to a large wet area. It looked like a pond that had to be crossed. I checked it out, trying to make a decision. My boots were waterproof and I could see the far side of it, so I decided to cross. Actually, I was afraid to walk around it because I was terrified about becoming disoriented. The foot trail stopped at the beginning of the mud and then picked up again on the other shore. I carefully waded in and kept my eyes focused on the tracks across the pond. It was a mistake. I started to sink into the mud.

"Fuck!" I shouted. "I'm in fucking quicksand!!!!" I felt my boots get swallowed up. "I'm going to perish here unless I can get out of this shit!" Then I had to do something. I had the rifle in one hand and now I had to save the backpack from being swallowed up in the mud. The two white bread sandwiches were in the backpack. I might have to eat those fucking sandwiches. What should I do? I could throw either the rifle or the backpack back to the dry edge of the sinking gunk, but not both. I decided to be thrifty and tossed the gun onto the dry grass, while the backpack and I became immersed in the vilest crap I had ever taken a bath in. Was this the end I had envisioned? Would I ever see my children again? I began to cry. Then I thought, as long as the sandwiches were history, plus everything in the backpack was muddied, maybe I should concentrate on saving myself. I was able to flip my body over like a turtle would do—I had seen upended turtles flip back to normal. I did it. Now I was in the gunk on my belly. I managed to keep my mouth above mud. I crawled to the so-called bank, hoisted myself on it and waited for the vultures which had been circling above to check me out.

Lots of time went by. I did not become unconscious, but I was dazed and confused. I prayed in two languages—English and Princess. "Please help me, honey," I moaned. "You're going to need me to cook for you, etc." I was thinking about my algae-infested swimming pool when I felt a hand on my back.

"What are you doing—you're covered with mud!" My husband stood over me, grinning like any self-respecting male chauvinist would have done. "You did good—you kept the gun dry!"

"What about me? I was near death!"

"No, I don't think so. Maybe you got a little chilled, but we can thaw you out in a few hours. By the way, I got my second animal."

"Gee, I'm glad. What do we do now?"

"The guide's going to take us back to camp. It's about ten miles—can you walk?"

"Sure, but I'm freezing and my clothes are soaked with mud, so I probably will die with my boots on—they will only take about two days to dry out and you can give them to your next woman."

"Listen, the guide says he'll take you back to camp on the ATV so you can clean up. I'll join the guys and we'll get back OK."

"What about our kills?"

"Oh, the guide has it all handled—all the parts of the four animals that they keep are already strapped on the vehicle."

"What about the parts they don't keep?"

"You see those flying predators up over your head?"

"Oh, those vulture creatures?"

"They're natural scavengers. They keep the landscape clean and neat. Except for the bones—they don't eat the bones."

"That's, uh, good."

So I got the bumpiest ride of my life as the guide, the carcasses and I were transported back to camp. Along the way I counted about eighteen sets of animal skeletons and about forty erratics—some of them the size of Chicago. I thought it was fortunate that I didn't have to consult the compass after all—it was somewhere on my arm, but right then I couldn't find it. All I could think about was the allure of that one shower in the one structure that was the bathing facility for everyone in the camp. They let me use it first because I was the filthiest. Also, word had gotten around that I had filled my quota of two caribou in one half hour. Nobody seemed to care that I had nearly died from anxiety.

That evening I saw the Northern Lights while going to the bathroom behind the big tent. I was doing it near a strategically placed tree, just like a dog would do—only a dog wouldn't know to look up at the sky. The green and blue waving bands of light were spectacular. They were so hypnotic a sight that after I pulled up my pajama bottoms, I stayed out there for a half hour at least. In the distance I could hear the sounds of men pissing, but I didn't care. I was one of the guys now.

Chapter 20
THE ALLURE OF PINSTRIPES AND POPCORN

When my husband and I weren't doing hunting, traveling, socializing, chain sawing[7] or bickering, there was always baseball. We both looked forward to the end of spring training and the launch of the season on Opening Day. How lucky I was to be married to a man who shared my fervor regarding this great American pastime. It was hard to tell who was more crazed about the game, but we had differing ways of enjoying it. I wasn't typical of my generation of women, but I love to tell my story about how I got to be such a nutcase of a baseball fan, and this is my chance.

❋❋❋

I have loved watching professional baseball since the age of five. My youthful enthusiasm for the sport seems to have been spawned during my years of growing up in a household where I was the child of two hard-working parents. Although I was the apple of my mother's eye, I was a precocious youngster. That's a tactful way of saying that I was an overzealous toddler—a handful. It is evident from my recollections that my demanding nature was an impediment to my parents' need for some sort of relief—like a day off from minding me. My father had a harrowing business routine, as did most struggling business owners of his day. Instead of spending a relaxing weekend afternoon with his best buddy, he seems to have been cajoled into taking me off my mother's hands on the only day of the week when she could give the house a thorough cleaning. I'm certain she cleaned the house more efficiently without me underfoot. Daddy must have felt forced to take me to watch the Cubs at Wrigley Field in Chicago because he didn't know what else to do with me. Babysitters were scarce in those years and his solution seems fairly enlightened when I think about it today. Tending little kids was women's work then, but taking a daughter to a ballgame? Brilliant!

I have clearer memories of the family routine after my brother came along when I was eight. The birth of a second child gave Mother the opportunity to be a stay-at-home housewife where she evidently lost her ability to force my father to do anything he didn't want to do. However, it was too late for him to avoid bringing me to ballgames for other reasons. Ticket prices for youngsters were cheap or even free back then. Also, I had become an authority on how I should be entertained and had convinced my father that it was his obligation to continue my education as a baseball enthusiast. His recourse was to include me as a member of a very select group—his four closest friends and the two of us. I liked being the sole juvenile in attendance in a coveted box seat along the first base line.

In those days before television came on the scene, avid North Sider Chicagoans who desired to see real players in action went to Wrigley Field and rooted for their beloved Cubbies no matter how well the team performed. Looking ahead to the present, I don't think much about that has changed. Anyway, Daddy got used to having me around during his afternoons out with the boys. Any discomfort he might have suffered was lessened as soon as we arrived at the old ballpark—that timeless icon of Chicago real estate—the house that chewing gum built—Wrigley Field. Not only did I become a really dedicated baseball fan—I developed an appetite for anything and everything edible that the vendors sold as they cruised up and down the aisles, shouting their selections. Between those juicy hot dogs (no mustard for me, of course) and the roar of the spectators whenever one of the players did something spectacular, I got hooked on the whole scene. I don't remember the conversations because this all happened so long ago, but I can imagine in my reconstructing mind how they might have gone:

"Daddy, can I have another hot dog?"

"What, you just ate one a half hour ago—aren't you full?"

"But Daddy, I love those red hot dogs and Mommy's don't taste as good! Daddy, Daddy, PLEEEEZE!" My begging usually worked, although sometimes an inning would go by before I had my way.

"I'll get you one at the Seventh Inning Stretch," Daddy would mutter while avoiding the stern looks in the eyes of his friends. None of them had cute little girls like me, but they could spot a manipulation routine a mile away.

"Why do we have to wait until the Seventh, Daddy? The hot dog guy is right over there in the next row!"

"Because that's when I feel like it. Leave me alone, will you? Lookee, Andy Pafko's coming to the plate! See how he stands in the batters' box—watch how he swings at the ball!"

I looked at my father's companions and I noticed they were temporarily fixated on the action in the field, so I tried a different approach. "OK, I love Andy Pafko, Daddy, but I'm tired of sitting here—it's so hot out today—oh, can I have a Coca Cola?"

"Oh, dammit, Pafko struck out!"

"How about an ice cream cone—I'm hot, Daddeeee!!!!"

Eventually Daddy gave up trying to get me to shut up before the seventh inning and I was finally indulged. However, as soon as my feelings of satisfaction had worn off, I would stare at the fans in the stadium and ask my dad if I could take an empty seat in the first row so I could be closer to the players. He always said absolutely not, so I would wait for his attention to be redirected and then I would stand up and walk along the aisle to the next section of box seats.

"Didn't I tell you to stay here?" Daddy would bellow when I was naughty.

"Daddy, I'm not sitting—I'm just standing and looking!"

"Well, come back here right now!"

I'd humbly obey him, of course, because the other guys were watching, but I still had to have my say.

"You're not giving me any attention—you're just talking to your friends!"

"We're discussing the game. Grownups get to have discussions. Children have to be seated and quiet. Watch the game."

"I am watching the game. The catcher just yelled at that guy with the mask!"

"That's the umpire. Players like to argue."

"Oh, like you and Mommy do whenever————"

"That's enough out of you!"

I know that this type of scenario as I have just described must have happened because how else could I possibly have become such an ardent baseball fan? The young male ballplayers fascinated me. I thought Andy Pafko and Phil Cavaretta, in particular, were kind of cute—Pafko with his tousled hair and Cavaretta, with his handsome features. I couldn't help myself—they were both better-looking than my father and they were so obviously the objects of love and adulation in those steamy summer days of Chicago in the forties. My girlfriends all had pictures of glamorous movie queens on their walls, but I had cut out pictures of my favorite Cubs players and put them into a baseball scrapbook. My personal ambitions were unreal, but they were all mine. I realized that they would never have me as an actual player on any sports team, but I did have a fantasy that I could be a baseball radio announcer some day in the distant future. I was just a bit ahead of my time.

I have to supply this background because it is a lead-in to my adaptation of life in Kerhonkson with my husband, who had become a New York Yankees fan as soon as he left Chicago and moved to Manhattan.

✳✳✳

In 1995, the year of our marriage, my husband invested in one of those newly designed small satellite dishes so we could get reception in our sheltered location in the foothills of the Catskill Mountains. Our neighbors to the southwest of us still had one of those huge dishes which occupied a large area of their side lawn. I would have hated having that big ugly thing invading my garden. Now we enjoyed a fairly clear picture on a 17-inch screen television set in the small living room. The TV was positioned diagonally in front of the bookcases and smack under the elk horns, just to the left of the huge black wood stove. I had never before seen such an imposing structure planted in the midst of an important room—installed there permanently for the sole purpose of warming up a house. With its black metal angled twelve-inch diameter tubing snaking up the living room wall, it dominated our living space and served as the heating system for the first and second floors. I named it the iron monster. We watched TV while sitting on the sleeper sofa nestled against the yellow wall across from the monster, where we could hear the crackling of the firewood and the whoosh as one spent piece of wood crashed against another. As soon as the Yankee game came on my husband would take his seat in his proprietary cushion, while I was free to fidget on the remainder of the three-seated sofa. I preferred my spot because it was close to the outside door which led to the little front porch. In case the heat got too much for me, I was only an arms-length from being able to open the door to get some air. On cool days or nights, we would have extra logs handy so that we could keep the roaring fire going without having to go to the trouble of starting all over with kindling. Soon the heat of the stove had me sweating like a starting pitcher winding up for his one-hundredth pitch.

"Don't you think it's a bit too warm in here?" I would quiz my baseball-loving hero while searching about his face to see if his sweat glands were operating.

"Yes, it is warm in here, honey, would you rather we turned on the radiators?"

"I guess not—they make all sorts of clanging noises and I don't want to be a pain in the butt."

"Watch the game—you'll come to love the money we're saving on heating oil."

"I love it already. Can we go to the real Yankees' stadium in the Bronx with the money we're not spending?"

"Any time you want, honey, any time you want. I'll find a date that works and we'll get tickets. We can have breakfast on the road and go to a day game. We'll have fun."

He always calmed me down and I became accustomed to having an overheated living room. I also began to treasure those times when we began to reminisce during the commercials. He glowed about New York players he had admired while I reminded him that I had been present the last time the Cubs had been in a World Series. That was in 1945 and since then the Yankees had been in more championship games than any other major league team in history. I loved watching the game and I fell into my own comfort zone where I could nearly scream to my heart's content over some heart-stopping shoe-string catch, so long as I refrained from doing the play by play. My husband preferred the official announcer to my own brand of chatter. I had come to the point where I really wanted the Yankees to win, but I still secretly wished we could have been watching it somewhere else, like the bleachers of a ballpark on a nice September day with a warm wind blowing steadily. I couldn't sit still on that sofa for the whole game.

"Honey, I'm so hot in here—I'm opening the living room door for just a few minutes!"

"Don't let too much cold air come in—oh, wow, Paul O'Neill's got a 3 and 1 count on him—come on, now, are you watching this or not?"

"I'm watching—I'm watching! I'm sweating, I'm sweating. Are you going to make some popcorn?"

"Yaah, as soon as the inning's over."

"OK, dear, I want just a little bit of your popcorn—you make such wonderful popcorn—it's better than what they have in the movie theatres and much cheaper!"

"Quiet!"

"Sorry, honey!"

"O'Neill struck out. I'll make some popcorn now."

"Don't put salt on the batch before I take my portion!"

"Well, then you have to get up off the couch and come into the kitchen and grab it."

"Of course, I wouldn't think of letting you have to isolate my non-blood-pressure-increasing little bit of nutrition."

"I like salt."

"I didn't mean to infer anything negative. I'm coming to get my treat." I rise from my cushion, my torso aching from sitting in an awkward position, and swiftly saunter into the kitchen to measure out my allotment of the popcorn batch. He's always in a hurry because God Forbid he should miss ten seconds of the beginning of the next inning. If I don't act swiftly, my territorial mate will nonchalantly sprinkle a torrent of salt on my requisitioned portion. Fortunately, he always lets me serve myself first so that he can enjoy his more gluttonous share free of guilt.

Like magic, just prior to the start of the first pitch of the next inning, he comes back into the living room toting a giant-sized stainless steel bowl of amazingly popped corn. It smells better than the lobby of the ten-screen movie house in Kingston—maybe because it seems to compete successfully with the smoky aroma emanating from the ashes in the catch panel of our wood stove. I enjoy eating my sweetheart's highly oiled puffy kernels, even though after indulging them I have to pick through my bridgework with a small version of a bottle brush in order to avoid serious dental discomfort.

As soon as my teeth feel unencumbered, I turn my attention to the game, but it is dragging at this point. I wish the guy on the mound would stop glaring at the runner on first and just throw the next pitch. He's unlikely to execute a pick-off play successfully, in my opinion, since everybody in the world knows that the man on first is toying with him, trying to distract him from locating his curve ball down and away, or whatever. Because of my vast experience, I know a great deal about how players bluff and go through the routine so that the pitcher gets all fuzzy about the base-runner's intentions. Besides, the time has arrived for me to execute my own move.

"Thanks for making the popcorn, honey," I sigh, as I sidle up to the sports fan next to me, trying to get some display of affection. I squeeze his arm playfully and rearrange myself in order to extract a kiss.

"Why are you getting on top of me? The score is tied!"

"I'm not on top of you—I'm just squeezing your elbow."

"Well don't do it during baseball! Watch the game!"

"I am watching the game! They're changing pitchers!"

"They're bringing in a left-hander!"

"Why can't I squeeze you while the players are gathered around the mound?" He doesn't answer, transfixed as he is while the manager trudges back to the dugout with his head down. Finally, I get my kiss, but it's a token. I realize I'm just feeling restless because even an avid baseball fan has the right to be bored once in awhile when the game becomes a contest of egos and strategies and the announcers start to talk about their kids or some old statistics to fill in the time.

I give up trying to get affection from the man of the house— the ruler of the sofa. I know I'll get it later, and especially if the Yankees win, because that will put him in one of his better moods. You see, a true baseball fan—especially a guy—knows his priorities. Besides, I've got my own priorities. I love watching Paul O'Neill move around the base path. That new guy, Derek Jeter is cute too.

I conclude that there is very little difference between the true blue sports fans of the forties in Chicago and the loyal-to-the-core sports fans of modern New Yorkers. Maybe there are slight variations in the degree of their emotional responses to the drama of the game. Some folks are more moody and caught up in the blood of it than others. I recall that my father's good humor went missing if the Cubs were losing, and now, in the nineties, if the Yankees appear to be going into free-fall, my spouse can swiftly lose his loving feeling. If I were to corner him later on and ask why he gets so worked up over a mere game, he will tell me that it is in his nature—that if he cuts himself he will bleed pinstripes.

As for me, I just like the whole baseball thing, because it's not only exciting, it's romantic. The more my husband tries to shrink himself into an untouchable ball of flesh on his side of the couch where he can second-guess the umpires' calls ad nauseum, the more I want to squeeze him and cover his anatomy with kisses. I'm not sure why baseball is such a turn-on for me. The best explanation I have is that when he seems unattainable I want to make a conquest.

Eventually the game concludes and we get back into our own heads and prepare to trudge upstairs to bed, but not before he demonstrates to me once again how to turn the fire down safely and where the tools and mitts are stored. He knows that I am capable of repeating the details of every single inning, but does he have confidence that I will remember the safety rules? Not a chance.

As the last of the popcorn dishes and utensils are scrubbed clean and the time-honored old dedicated popping pot is stored, it is sleepy time. I still harbor the feeling that I could stay awake for hours, but then I keep forgetting that I'm not a restless juvenile any longer. Instead I'm a restless aging married woman with a worn-out sports fanatic for a mate. "This is true love," I say to myself, "this is how a good marriage happens after you get over the crunch time of the so-called period of adjustment."

I'm still in love, I think, but unlike that initial courtship whirl, I don't hear a single bell or siren song—just the zipping down of my husband's pants as he undresses and the slamming down of the upstairs window in the bedroom because that room has gotten cold from the wind. The wood stove heating system isn't perfect.

I do lie awake for a half hour or so thinking about my love affair with this third husband of mine. The comparisons ramble around in my thoughts. When I recall my single life to my current life with its gift of spousal partnership, there is no contest at all. On this particular evening I get the whole picture—really get it. I have in my autumn years indeed hit a home run with the bases loaded. It doesn't seem problematic at all that once in awhile one of the two players makes an error.

Chapter 21
THE DOG AND THE GARDENER—PART ONE

For those of you who couldn't figure it out, I am the gardener. The garden is the area within our acreage that has been tampered with by me. The dog is not my dog—it is not even our dog—it is simply, The Dog. The Dog got here because I couldn't acquire a fence around my garden.

It all began one day in May. I had cleared the big side hill of unchecked growth, including twenty miles of poison ivy vines, and now I began serious planting. It had to be decorative and practical, but I figured that I could insert some hybrid roses in a strategic place at the bottom of the hill. I had agonized about the cost, but finally acquiesced and paid one hundred seventy-five dollars of my own money to purchase several boxed rosebushes. These were the kind that required the aspiring gardener to dig the proper holes to the proper depth, place the proper fertilizer at the proper place, and then do the mulch and water routine as per the instructions on the box. Soon growth would proceed and yield pleasure to the eyes and noses of visitors. We hadn't had any visitors for a month and didn't expect any, since we lived where no one with any intelligence would spend any significant effort to get there. Nevertheless, I finished the planting and came into the house to attend to my bloodied fingers and ruined manicure. The man of the house was in his study, but called out to acknowledge my entry.

"Finished?"

"Sort of," I answered listlessly while searching for a package of bandages in one of the junk drawers.

"My wife used to plant roses—I don't imagine you found them under the weeds yet." He spoke from his room, since he saw no need to get up from his desk chair merely to exchange a few unexciting remarks with the one other person in the household.

"I'm your wife," I reminded him, "but no, I didn't find any trace of anything cultivated previously, although I did get some sticky burrs on my jeans—they were mixed in with the brambles where you said there once was a vegetable patch."

"Uh huh. Lots of those sticky burrs out there." His voice trailed off from a low pitch to an inaudible mutter, but I had trained myself to fill in what he had probably said.

Then I made my special announcement, counting on the possibility that he cared. "Next week I expect to see some gorgeous hybrid teas where the poison ivy used to prevail."

"Oh, did you use gloves, like I told you?"

"Yes, I used gloves, but I had to take them off because I needed to feel where the thorns were."

"You're not sensitive, I hope."

"If you mean about sensitivity to poison ivy, the answer is Nope!"

"Well, what other sensitivity could there be?"

"Oh, I'm sensitive about whether I can really grow roses, whether I should be gardening rather than getting my nails done, you know, the trophy wife routine."

"You're too old to be a trophy wife."

"That was another item on my sensitivity list."

I didn't hear any further remarks from him, so I went about my business. I put my tools away and decided a soaking bath was in order. After luxuriating in almond-scented bath beads, I began to think about my new gardening hobby. I had purchased one book about growing roses and realized that I should have dug the holes a little deeper. I had to forgive myself for going too shallow because the soil in our area was full of rocks—tiny rocks, average rocks and rocks that were so large their dimensions were unknown. These latter ones were best left by themselves, since I had been warned by my husband that some of the underground stones in our part of the foothills were deposited there by glaciers.

"When you get the big shovel," he emphasized, "don't injure yourself if you hit stone and it won't budge. What you have uncovered could be the size of a Toyota."

I don't know why he picked on that automobile brand to describe a natural ingredient of our landscape, but the imagery that it did create served as a constant reminder to me that I could not always control my environment. I made a mental note to add underground stones to my list of things I couldn't control.

I went to sleep peacefully, thinking, "At least I did the best I could when I put those bushes in those holes."

A week passed during which I visited my precious bushes about six times a day, monitoring the new growth and drooling over the emerging petals because they were like children to me. One day, at just about twilight, I was rewarded with the sight of five nearly open blossoms of such a glorious shade of peach that I felt that my separation from my former townhouse with its high pile wall-to-wall carpeting of that same shade was complete. I had always loved peach anything, so I had purposely chosen plants that the packaging indicated would bloom with the most vivid peach-hued flowers ever hybridized. Before I went to sleep, I vocalized a promise that was difficult for me, but I did it anyway:

"Honey, tomorrow morning I'm going to take photos of the new blooms—just like you taught me—shallow depth of field and compensation for too much sun—the whole ball of wax."

"Good. I'm going to the gym, so I won't be here to help you. That means that you and only you are going to try out the camera that has remained in the box it came in since I got it for you."

"Are you suggesting that I ignored your gift last April?"

"Of course not. But why was the factory seal still on the box and why did the top of the package have fresh dust?"

"I've been busy."

"Doing the heavy cleaning on the picture window in the bedroom? I think I was able to see through it this morning."

"Not so! You act like I never have any client work to do."

"Sorry, I heard your computer boot up, but I thought you were playing a solitaire game on it."

I shut up because I had been playing a solitaire game the whole day before—my excuse was that it rained. All my energies were focused on those budding hybrid teas—peach blossoms with nectars so sweet and colors so vivid they would win prizes. The evening passed and in the morning, awakened by the six-o-clock bugle call of my husband's thirty-year-old alarm clock, I raised my head and torso up with a feeble stretching exercise. It was a promising day of fine weather. The morning sun had worked its way through our bedroom picture window—the part that I had squirted clean a few days earlier—in order to check for uninvited rodents. I had noticed that for several mornings in a row pesky creatures were darting in and out along the flower beds near the kitchen window and that some intruder had dug up most of the tulip bulbs and "displanted" a bunch of new seedlings. Sure enough, two squirrels were down there, eyeing the scattered upended little green starter plants, neither of the suspect rodents appearing to be concerned about my garden design plans.

I heard my husband calling me to breakfast. He always dressed and shaved quickly. I always dressed and handled my morning grooming slowly. First I would satisfy myself that it was really daytime and that he wasn't the type to wait around for a sleep-in wife. My routine was to call out: "I'm up! I'm up!" I always announced those words as I rolled over one more time in the comfy bed, putting the pillow over my face. Then I did arise and called out louder: "I'm really up now—putting my clothes on!" He usually responded with his favorite phrase:

"I'll alert the media."

"Husband, get me coffee."

"Get out of bed, woman, and make me pancakes."

"First, I have to check for the roses."

"You're not doing that before breakfast."

"Why not?"

"Because you'll get lost down there."

"No I won't."

"Yes you will, and if I see you peeking before cooking, I'm going to hide your camera and your part of the newspaper."

I have to explain something here—we both enjoyed reading the daily newspaper over breakfast. Every morning the carrier would toss it onto the driveway—sometimes where we could find it without a search of the surrounding underbrush and sometimes not. Usually my husband went to retrieve it because he was the more energetic at 6:30AM. We took turns reading the various sections—he got the first section on odd days and I got the first section on even days. Fairness and thrift and marital compromise trumped my natural desire to hog all the more interesting news all the time.

However, on this occasion, when he slipped out the back door to get the paper, I peeked out the dining room window to get a first look at the blooms. I couldn't see any blooms. That's when I knew I had to take advantage of him when he retreated after breakfast to our hygiene library. I shot out the front door and ran down the front steps to look at the roses. A rude shock awaited me. There, along the neat row of freshly planted bushes, rose greenish brown stems, a few green thorns of fresh growth and one small bud that was still closed. In the night a poltergeist had come and removed all the roses and all the rosebuds and left a straggly mess of torn stems and broken dreams. I retreated to the confines of the living room and lay down on the sofa, mourning my loss. He had come into the room and discovered me weeping on the toss pillow.

"Why are you crying?"

"My roses were eaten last night."

"Well, the young deer need to fill up—they have to grow too, you know."

"But why MY roses?" Blubbering, I tried to make sense of the universe that was my whole world at the moment.

"It's not personal, you know. They run, they grow, they shit, they eat, they screw. You do it too. That's the order of things. Let's finish breakfast and then go food shopping. I require fresh vegetables and I've made out a list."

"Can't we get a fence to keep the deer out? I've been begging you for a fence!"

"We have five hundred frontage feet and where are you going to put an eight-foot high fence? Across the driveway that we have to drive up to get to the house? Are you nuts? A fence will cost ten thousand dollars—maybe more!"

"Well, are you telling me that I moved all the way here from Illinois and I can't have any roses?"

"No. You can have roses. Just not outside."

"Well, the ones I want are outside ones."

"You want to cough up ten thousand? No, wait a minute—I don't even want a fence that you pay for. Forget the fence. However, what the apple growers do is have dogs that chase away the deer. You want a dog?"

"I've never had a pet before because my parents wouldn't let me when I was a kid and then my kids wouldn't take care of one, so we just—- oh, we just kept arguing and, uh,—why are you looking at me like that?"

"I asked you if you wanted a dog and you're giving me your life story."

"Well, OK, do I want a pet that—"

"No! Not a pet! I'm talking about a working dog—not a pet."

"I didn't know they worked. Do they have a union?"

"Dogs chase deer. All we need is an invisible fence. That will cost over a thousand, but I'll agree to get one if you train the dog."

"I can't even train you."

"Yes or no?"

"OK—where should we shop for a dog?"

"At the SPCA—we'll go there next week. We can adopt a two-year-old female."

"Why a two-year-old female?"

"Because that's the energetic year of a young dog and a male would piss against all the plants. A female will go wherever we train her to go."

"You mean keep the dog outside?"

"Sure, that's where you keep a working dog. We'll get a long-haired pooch."

"Oh. Well, I'll do anything to have a few roses."

"Wait a minute—it'll be your job to feed the dog and take her to the vet and give her doggie medicine and clean her kennel and give her attention when she needs it."

"My job, my job, everything's my job. All of a sudden this sounds like a big deal."

"Forget it, then."

The dog-as-garden-savior subject was dropped for a few days until I discovered that all my hosta plants had been munched down within inches of their roots. Ditto all the young rhododendron plants. I sat in the midst of an intended grove of shrubs that wasn't going to be a grove any time soon and cried for an hour. The only plant that seemed to avoid being devoured by an invisible herd that came in the night was the lowly mushroom. When I began having nightmares that resembled bad science fiction films, I knew I'd have to change my wayward ways.

Chapter 22
THE DOG AND THE GARDENER—PART TWO

I began to notice a distinct pattern to my resistance to adapting to my new country life. Whenever my husband had lost patience with me for refusing to take up any solution he had proposed to a problem I had wailed about, his method was to utter those two ominous words, "Forget it." Now I was up against it—facing my fears of looking foolish and succumbing to the wise ways of my experienced husband. He had undergone years of hacking out an interesting existence as a man who could cope like a pilgrim and govern his turf like a feudal lord, now with me as his only subject. I was the one who desired a garden to rival the Rockefeller estate and he was the one who had actually interviewed apple farmers. My obsession had been mushrooming for that whole planting season. Plus I had finally understood in my gut where that expression had come from. I brought up my concern about the idea of getting a dog at breakfast next morning.

"Honey, I figured out what is driving my gardening obsession."

"You don't have to explain yourself," he commented, reaching for his sixth cup of coffee. "All women have to have some obsessions, otherwise how would husbands feel superior?"

"I've never heard you admit to feeling superior before! Every time I mention your arrogance, you ignore me!"

"Well, who has more right to be arrogant than me?"

"I think it's 'than I.' "

"I know you love gardening. The yard looks very nice. Let's find just the right dog."

"That brings up an important issue for me. I'm not sure I can handle a real active dog."

"Listen, babe (he referred to me as 'babe' whenever he had an extra piece of wisdom to throw in), listen up! Dogs have been domesticated for thousands of years, even if you haven't."

"You told me you liked a wild woman."

"I do. Can you finish cleaning the kitchen?" He wrinkled his nose in a pleading manner when he needed a favor. It was his turn to do the kitchen and he had to attend to another matter that morning.

"I'll do the kitchen and let's go adopt a deer-chasing puppy."

✳✳✳

Next week we adopted a two-year-old mutt. She looked like a mix of Huskie, Rottweiler, Akita and German Shepherd all rolled into one crazy canine. She seemed to have a great deal of energy. I had no experience on how to handle her, so I asked the SPCA lady about thirty questions until she got tired of answering me and left the room. Before we signed the papers, we knelt before our new puppy's cage and introduced ourselves. She had a name that she answered to—Geraldine. I wanted to name her Rosebud, but she wouldn't respond to that, so I gave in. I was now the proud mistress of a hyperactive animal that, as time would tell, could not be trained to do anything but run after other animals.

Soon after she was given the shock therapy that forever reminded her to remain within the electrified perimeter, we began
to relax a bit and let her do her job. However, her version of her
purpose in life differed from ours. We began finding deceased
victims of her lust on our various lawns and pathways. I tallied
them up. She was the proximate cause of death of many voles, a
woodchuck, two possums, one box turtle, a red fox, three squirrels, a chipmunk and several baby birds which had tumbled from
nests. Her most challenging achievement was the wounding of one
skunk which had apparently escaped but left its souvenir aroma
around our picnic table for more than a week. She treed one stray
kitten for two days until we got our tallest ladder out and helped it
get down. First we had to leash our barking stalker to a tree hundreds of feet away so the kitten would have a sense of security.

Geraldine howled every night and when I tried to pet her,
she would back away and do a little jig in a circle around me, in
a special doggie dance of her own. She refused to bond with me
normally and gave me the kind of grief that I used to suffer with
an obstinate child. We bought an outside feeder that would hold
three days worth of food, and we bought the best dog chow on
the market, but as soon as we filled it, she ate all three days of it
without stopping to digest it. We had to resort to giving her one
day's food at a time, which meant we couldn't leave her overnight
at all, so if we wished to take a few days of vacation, we had to hire
a special dog sitter. She left her feces everywhere and chewed off
the little doggie sweater I bought for her in about fifteen minutes.
When I first told my husband about the purchase of the sweater he
had a good laugh.

"Did you really think that mutt was going to let you put clothing on her?"

"Why not—doesn't she ever feel cold? I'm always cold around
here in the evenings."

"First, she's got a long coat of thick hair and you don't. Second, she's a wild animal and you, uh, you, well, I'm afraid to make the comparison because you might slap my face. She's not some house poodle that you dress up. Wait and see."

I hated that he knew so much more about animals than I did and that he had an amazing track record of predictions. That five dollar dog sweater was another lesson I had to learn. I felt inadequate to the task of truly bonding with her, but I decided to put up a pretty good front as a serious dog owner. I followed the rules in the aged book for dog owners that my husband retrieved from a very high shelf. Those rules spelled out the importance of keeping the dog healthy. When it was time to go to the vet I had to put Geraldine in a special cage which fit in the hatchback portion of my car. There was a real safety concern about transporting such a frisky animal because if she wasn't confined in an enclosure she would have jumped all over me, most likely while I was making my way over the Shawangunk mountain pass.

The vet's clinic was a renovated nineteenth century farmhouse in the center of New Paltz. I actually enjoyed going there because I felt a sense of nostalgia—like the mommy I once was taking my baby for its shots. It was at this pet care establishment where I forever discarded my reputation as a lost cause pet handler and gained some self-respect as a good dog mother. I had selected the best animal center in the county and paid for Geraldine's care with my own money. However, getting that energetic creature in and out of that cage and onto the path that led to the porch of the clinic was some challenging feat. The trickiest part was to attach her leash before she could dash away from me because she could have wound up in Poughkeepsie, a half hour away.

That mutt had to sniff every foot of the way along the pavement from the car to the door of the office and she was stronger than me, but I gave it my all. My manner was extremely professional. To be more accurate, I had the vet's entire office staff hoodwinked. I knew my untrained dog might try to eat parts of the other animal clients in the waiting room, so I held so firmly to the leash and her collar that they thought I was a dog trainer. I never told any of them that the dog had trained me or that I was a lawyer who worried about somebody suing me for having an out-of-control attack animal. The Dog and I got away with the fraud for all the years we visited that vet's office.

With all the trials and challenges thrown at me, I have to admit—Geraldine did chase away most of the deer. My reward for learning how to live in her world and love her was that I did get to keep most of the following years' crops of roses, plus an amazing amount of other types of plants that usually succumbed to grazing deer who continually feasted on peoples' favorite flowers and shrubs. We country folks referred to it as the green smorgasbord for all comers. I was able to dispense with the other tricks gardeners used. I found out that the gardening crews for the big Duchess County mansions had erected stakes next to the flowers with little holders for cakes of soap to protect their rose beds. It was believed that the scent kept the deer away. When I tried that technique it hadn't worked well for me—the baby deer knocked the soap over and defied Geraldine's howled warning. They were that hungry and fearless. To this day I believe that during my rosebush loving years there were deer roaming around Ulster County that smelled from Irish Spring®.

I didn't win any gardening prizes, but I should have won a prize for learning to be an intellectual match for a wild animal.

We had to get used to the howling at night. No neighbors ever complained—they were too far away from our habitation. Apparently, Geraldine's parentage wasn't completely understood, and I became convinced that she was part wolf. She even looked like one. I had always enjoyed the untamed wilderness tales by rugged authors such as Jack London, but I didn't think their stories would come true for me that way. Geraldine had me for an owner—I could never claim that I had her. Which was the way my marriage worked usually, so I took it in stride.

I have to be complete with this story, so get a load of this happy ending: Geraldine, the working dog, took care of my extensive garden for eight years and had a fine old time of it running all over and around the garden patches, walkways, lawns, stepping stones, shrub barriers and little concrete statues like they belonged to her alone. Eventually, we decided to sell the property before we each died from some maintenance injury, falling tree limb or storm-related stress. One of my husband's shooting buddies had been able to bond with Geraldine easily and it became fairly clear that they loved each other. Every time he came over, she jumped into his arms and made me feel like some outsider. She had found a new owner to indulge her and take her off our hands and we soon found a buyer for the place.

I still have dreams about ghosts that steal roses in the middle of the night.

Chapter 23
HOW MARRIED PEOPLE TALK TO EACH OTHER

After a number of years of the bliss that I expected when I re-married, I noticed that things got a little frosty between the two of us occasionally. Was it me? Was it him? Was it inevitable? I thought about all those implicit vows and reasoned that after two divorces, a woman doesn't rack up points for all those additional rounds of contested marital issues. I had promised myself that this third one was for keeps. Thus, my reasoning went, any ensuing problems also had to be mine and I had to do some more adjusting.

Like a new house where the foundation begins to settle into the site, allowing a few cracks to appear, my body began to settle also and my physical checkups stopped being no-brainers. Another way of putting it is that after twelve years of marriage, I became twelve years more medically interesting. I had come out of a routine colonoscopy procedure with a fairly high probability that I'd be alive for awhile. The stuff that was done had me feeling punk and natu-rally I expected some coddling when I got home. I worried that my husband by that time might have forgotten his end of the basic cod-dling program. Sure enough, his manners failed him. It didn't mat-ter whether the failure was a case of bad memory or rusty karma—I still felt neglected. I can remember that setback to my confidence like it was yesterday. Hold on now—maybe my memory has tinkered with the time frame, because I think it was yesterday.

✳✳✳

172

I'm sitting on the living room sofa, shivering for no good reason except for my habit of shivering all the time when I'm inside our Florida house with the fans going.

I tell my husband, or rather ask my husband without the inflection that there's a question involved, "Honey, get me my sweater—I left it in your car."

"Get your own sweater."

"Why can't you be nice to me—I just came home from the clinic?"

"Whatever. I know."

"That's not the response I'd hoped for."

"Uh huh."

"So please? Bring me my sweater?"

"Whatever."

In short order he disappears and then reappears and a black cardigan is flung at my face. He goes into the kitchen to make himself a snack. I unwind the sweater from my neck and, since it was of soft material, I am not damaged and I put it on. He comes into the room chomping on a half bagel. I wish he had asked me if I wanted the other half. He sits down next to me on the stuffed sofa without saying howdedo. I'm used to it. If he suddenly became voluble, I would check his pulse or the alcoholic content of his various medications. Short uncommunicative words are his favorites. He opens his mouth. I strain my ears waiting for the next syllable. It comes. or rather, they come.

"Move over."

I realign my butt. I just got two words for the price of one. Love still reigns.

What about the word, whatever? When did it become a substitute for the term, "It's sort of all right with me and I don't really care." That one disrespectful word has been pressed into service as a way for the most taciturn and emotionally stifled to equivocate without fear of retaliation for something he or she said. I am beginning to realize the wisdom of this expression and cannot deny the virtues of brevity, even though I would have preferred verbosity.

My fantasy, of course, was different. In my dreams I wanted my husband to fawn all over me and wait on me hand and foot because that's what I would have done for him.

Suppose the shoe were on the other foot and <u>he</u> was the one who had just returned from the clinic:

"Honey," I whisper, "Are you OK?"

"I'm OK."

"Can I get you something?"

"Please don't hover over me—I'm OK."

"Well, would you like me to make dinner early?"

"I'm not hungry now. Please don't try to comfort me—I don't want it."

"Yes, dear, I'll leave you alone for awhile."

"Whatever."

This would be the script for about fifteen minutes. I can visualize the next scene: A masculine quaver enters the voice of my loved one and his lips curl with a hint of humility. He speaks in a much softer tone than I can ever muster:

"I didn't mean to be short with you."

"Of course not."

"I'll discuss what the doctor said in a few minutes."

"OK."

"I'm kind of down now."

"Well, can I————?"

"Stop. Don't go there."

"Go where?"

"Don't offer me tea and sympathy. I'm just not ready to get happy. I'll cheer up later."

Later does come eventually and he empties his emotions as only he can do—using fewer words than I would, but descriptive enough so that I know he's still a man and in control. Different married couples have different codes and it's important to get the signals right—even if the woman is enlightened. When the husband is holding back his feelings and the woman has to unlearn all the touchy feely therapy she once learned in order to get along with other people, it's all right. He's just not other people.

My mind whispers to me: Wait till he needs something.

I have learned a few things during my abundance of marriages. Spouses tend to relax their manners as the years go by. Rudeness replaces politeness. Grunts replace sighs. Half closed eyes replace bedroom eyes. Disputes can become animated. None of this trending downward conversation with one another means that the marriage is in trouble. It's true that we have learned to insult each other in increasingly graphic terms. Yet our bonds of matrimony have grown stronger as our checkbooks have become weaker. Mother always said that I would learn to love my husband more and more as our lives continued as one. So it took me a few years to prove she was right! I simply had to adapt her wisdom to the new ways and the kind of guy who would put up with me. I also had to learn the "marital code."

The marital code includes Frequently Uttered Words (F.U.W.) or Frequently Uttered Terms (F.U.T.) His FUW is "whatever" and FUT is "lay off", while my FUW is "overwhelm" and FUT is "what did you say?" Every couple should get along like we do, but watch out for those FUW's and FUT's.

My parents had a different marital code and as a child I never understood it or why it sounded so rough. They didn't have the term "whatever." That term is the current generation's catchall— a three-syllable comeback for the ignorant, the introverted, the super-arrogant and the dumbstruck. Here's my cynicism rearing its ugly head again. At least my parents had style—in an aggressive way that was apparently practiced back in the forties. My mother was bound by the old tradition, but wow, was she ever feisty! ("Feisty" is the feminist-influenced transformation of the term "high-strung.") Feistiness took certain forms. My father's FUT was a two-word maxim—my memory is true—I can still hear his voice uttering the two unambiguous words "shut up!" And her FUT comeback, according to my unrepressed memories of conversations way back then, was a three-parter—it was "You shut up!" Oh my, they had a great time together back in the good old days when divorce wasn't even a last resort for bitter connubial hook-ups—it was an institution reserved for the very rich and the very insane. Everyone else toughed it through by slugging it out verbally, early, often, and in front of the children when necessary.

I have finally reconciled my feelings about wives in my mother's generation with my worldview today. That reconciliation will come into play if and when I finally get really old and feeble.

Chapter 24
MONEY MISMANAGEMENT AND OTHER SELF-INFLICTED INJURIES— PART ONE

When we married and decided not to pool our wealth, I had to accept the new order of things. No longer would I be able to run my credit cards through the system in order to buy whatever my acquisitive heart desired, figuring out after the fact how to balance the books. We had worked out an unwritten contract with terms and conditions agreeable to him, even though I was the lawyer. The back-story of this drama bears revealing.

"You have a terrible habit of managing your finances," he would begin. "I can't believe that a tax attorney would be so careless." This statement and other similar pronouncements were daily reminders that I was being urged to rethink my version of the road to financial success.

"I know all that—I told you why I spent money—I was lonely and when I bought things for the house, well, those things kept me company."

"You mean like that teddy bear you dragged here? I'm your teddy bear now—what did you do with the toy one that can't hold a candle to me?"

"I lost it when we moved. It's somewhere."

"You don't need it. You don't need most of your possessions. You do need me."

"I know, the Beatles said it for all of us, "All You Need is Love.""

"I didn't mean that—I meant that here where we live—out in the country and in this house—there is no use for items like pedestals for unnecessary floral arrangements, coffee tables, three sets of china or antique ink stands. You should sell or give away this junk."

"You made me sell that designer Lucite piece that could have been a coffee table for us!"

"You did right to sell it—we have no room for a coffee table."

"I have nothing to put my coffee cup on when we sit on the sofa in the living room."

"I told you the rules around here—while in the living room—no camping!"

"Camping? You mean no food or snacky stuff when I watch TV, don't you? Everybody snacks in front of the TV."

"I didn't let my family eat in the living room—we ate in the dining room or in the kitchen, during mealtimes, of course."

"Is that why you never gain weight? I could try that approach."

"Try to see my point of view—what would you rather do? Look at tchochkes or take a trip to Alaska?"

"Well, it would be nice to have both, but before I married you, I was working very hard on my strategy of how to get rich. Then when we got engaged I decided that you might just be a pretty damned good shortcut! Can't a girl ever change horses in mid-stream?"

"You're not a girl any longer, and I'm not a horse. I'm going to help you with your money management. You can be comfortable and happy and content, or you can be a nervous wreck worrying about the stock market or your credit card debt—which is better?"

"I don't want your detached, cool, well-reasoned logic—I want your permission for me to ease off my old habits!" I need a gentle phase-out—not a kick in the ass!"

"A gentle phase-out? That sounds like something a psychologically screwed up weirdo or a politician would say—even a weasel wouldn't debase itself by thinking like that!"

"You are so hard! Did you get that way in the army? Who was your role model? I know who mine was!"

"I mean no disrespect to your deceased parents, but I'm afraid the habits you picked up from your upwardly mobile folks are the early warning signposts on the profligate road to bankruptcy."

"Why did you marry me?"

"Oh, I knew you were smarter than the condition of that balance sheet you showed me—you've already paid off all your debts and I see you've begun to save for the future—I know you can do it!"

"Don't you ever get bored from being right all the time? I've had to tell all my old friends that I married the perfect man and now I have to teach myself how to be humble. That's even harder than learning how to fool Mother Nature."

Some of his comments used to sting—especially the ones regarding my finances. I guess I worked hard at manufacturing glib comebacks, but even they often sounded lame. Those were days when my mental salve was to retreat to the kitchen where I could replay my own arguments in my head while I nosed around the cupboards for a favorite snack. My belief system included the knee-jerk response that there could be nothing worse than having to face reality without a bag of Doritos® or at least a handful of raisins.

Such reasoning actually did lead me to taking up gardening. Every time he hit me right in the old ego with his careful analysis of my flaws, I had to pick myself up by performing a chore, like transplanting a five foot shrub or preparing a new bed for some flowers I hadn't bought yet. There was a great payoff here—I got more exercise than I ever dreamed of and saved money I might otherwise have squandered. Although I worried that my lack of invading the shopping malls for bargains might injure the local economy, I had begun to realize that I might be better off dealing with my consumerist ways. While I was going through the transformation of becoming a miser, another brainstorm came to me and this time I didn't need anybody's advice.

It occurred to me that if I was going to fix one behavioral imperfection, why not go for two? "Give up the Doritos," my courageous mind shouted. "Hang onto the Doritos a little longer," my timid self shouted back." Then I did the math. For every snack of Doritos I would now deny myself, I would put fifty cents into a rainy day fund. It seemed simple enough. Not only would I save at the vending machines or checkout counters—I'd be working on my waistline at the same time! I was experiencing anxiety either way, so I might as well give myself an anxiety bonus.

As a model for better eating, I decided to emulate my better half. He was always on my case about my food choices, so I made some changes in my diet without mentioning it to him. Then, if he noticed, I could act smug, having picked up the art of it right out of his playbook. Soon vitamin-enriched cereal replaced the Doritos and grape tomatoes replaced canned fruit cocktail. After-dinner desserts became after-dinner cups of tea or low-calorie cider mixes. Instead of two eggs at breakfast, I had one egg every other day. I cut down on my portions and avoided creamed side dishes. After a week of this the routine got easier, but life wasn't exactly a bed of roses. I looked at our inventory of healthy food in half empty kitchen cabinets and wondered if I was turning into him. That would be going too far. Somehow I managed to keep some of my plump curves, which I always regarded as protection for my inner child. Nevertheless, my concerns spread from changes in eating habits to changes in wardrobe habits. I worried that I was becoming lazy about my maintenance of carefully coordinated clothing ensembles. This worry showed up when he gave me a Filene's gift certificate for $200.

"Honey, I appreciate this nice gesture, but I'm afraid to go into that store because they have such nice things."

"You deserve to buy yourself something—you've lost some weight and you look nice."

What was he telling me? That because I had stopped some of my frivolous spending and begun eating more veggies that I could get him to pop for my clothes? Why hadn't I figured that out earlier?

"I'm afraid that I won't be able to stop at $200 because I'll want to buy some new outfits."

"Just buy $200 worth. Make that your goal."

Wow, he had everything so down pat! Just spend $200. Well, Filene's had new jeans outfits and since I had become the counterpart of Mr. Rustic, I loaded up on them and omitted the accessorizing. There would not be any new belts, scarves, matching purses or beads to tie everything together. It was agony. I hated facing the pain of loss of serious detail shopping—that cold dose of medicine that didn't come in a jar or a bottle—sobriety for a spender.

The small amount of closet space allotted for my "dress" clothes was appropriate for how little I wore them. It no longer mattered to me that my few stylish outfits were inconveniently wedged behind my husband's assortment of work shirts and blue jeans. In cold weather he wore flannel shirts and in warm weather he wore tee shirts or polo shirts. Each item had to be finger-spaced and hung exactly right, like rows of soldiers lined up in a march. He knew that his space was outflanking mine, so he suggested I empty out another small closet in another room and use it for my overflow. My issue was not about the inconvenience of two separate closets, however—it was about wardrobe philosophy. Before I married him, I had become a product of the disposable culture, and even though we were the same age, he was a product of the retention culture.

On the morning after our wedding day, while packing up my stuff for the big move, we had a terrible fight over my old electric can-opener. I won't go into the details here, but I did give him an unrehearsed speech. It went something like the following, but I've cleaned it up a bit:

I began the discussion as though I were advising a client. "When two people of differing cultures unite in holy wedlock, it's better to get all the nitty-gritty disagreements out on the table."

"OK," he fumed, "we don't need your damned electric can-opener from your first damned marriage—I have plenty of hand-held can-openers!"

"Aha!" I exclaimed. "You've just made a unilateral decision that didn't involve me!"

"That's redundant—'unilateral' means—"

"Oh, shut up! Don't finish the sentence!" Then I reinforced my argument by starting to cry. That's when I learned that a tearful outburst didn't work with this man. The only thing that did work was carefully conceived logic. I cried some more.

"I can't stand this," he shouted, turning purple. "Keep your damned can-opener!" We kissed and made up because we were still in our pajamas.

He had brought me down to earth at the time, but just by a few centimeters. I needed to elevate his decision-making to square with my ideals, so I had to plot a strategy. I had been working on learning the art of compromise, but it was painful and required my doing most things his way for the first few months. However, as I gained credibility, I detected a subtle shift in my power and acted on it.

First, I forced him to discard his raggedy bath towels and replace them with new ones. We had disagreements over how thick a bath towel should be and our views resulted in a standoff. He went for thin and I preferred thick. His and hers towels took on a whole new meaning. He enjoyed ribbing me about using towels that took up an entire wash load and deposited half their volume in a clump of fluff in the lint-catcher of the dryer. I retaliated by calling his towels cheesy to the point of transparency. These were sobering discussions. I decided that if he wanted to play the game of who collected more household brownie points for brilliance of product selection, then I had a winning strategy to take him down a peg—a killer example: He was still darning his socks.

184

Perched on a special shelf in our bedroom was an old round candy tin containing his collection of darning needles, threads in varied socks colors for men, thimbles that would have made my grandmother envious, and a few pincushions that would have made my great-grandmother envious. That tin box occupied the whole of an architectural space I would rather have filled with a figurine or some other curio. His routine was to get to the sock darning task in the evening while watching TV, which seemed a good time for me to confront him:

"I didn't know anybody darned socks any longer."

"New socks cost money I would rather spend on something else,"

"Like a new reloading press?"

"Maybe."

"Have you looked in a store lately, like in the last few years? My socks are so cheap that I buy them in packages of six at a time. Of course, I can't wear wool, and I see that you prefer that."

"Wool is warmer and I hate shopping. Give me a good old catalog every time."

"Wool is scratchy and attracts moths. Shopping is fun, or at least it was fun."

"What's fun about it? It's not entertaining at all. When's the last time a saleswoman said to you, 'Hey, look at our new expensive designer dresses,' and you had a good laugh?"

"Well, I like to feel pretty, and don't start up on me with that silly song!"

"You are pretty. And don't go moving my darning equipment where I can't find it!"

"Do your friends from the gun club know you do sewing?"

He didn't answer. I discovered a couple of weeks later that he had bought himself packages of new socks and surreptitiously hidden them in his underwear drawer. That's the way he was. He would rarely admit I had any good ideas. I had to find out where my influence extended by careful observation. Yes, I did peek in the drawers of his bureau occasionally, but they were very furtive peeks. Each item of apparel was pressed and folded and mounted in stacks exactly ten inches high in designated spaces like a parking lot for shirts. He <u>was</u> perfect.

Chapter 25
MONEY MISMANAGEMENT AND OTHER SELF-INFLICTED INJURIES— PART TWO

I guess all married couples engage in animated conversations from time to time. I know we did whenever money or most any other issue arose. He had asked me if my parents ever taught me how to save for the future. I knew the answer right off the bat—my mother's future was the following week. She had carefully planned exactly when she'd be patronizing certain stores to get the best prices on new shoes and handbags. Then she would sneak them into the house and prepare her speech for my father. This was the culture. None of her friends seemed concerned about needing more closet space or larger homes. Nobody in our neighborhood grew their own tomatoes or went into a shed to milk a goat for beverages for the kids. Now my husband and I exchanged tales about our differing purchasing patterns. I had been a type of food shop-a-holic and often bought ingredients for recipes I never actually tried. They accumulated in my single woman's kitchen and in an additional cabinet I kept in my laundry room. He and his first wife were rubes, I thought. They grew apple trees and canned seventy quarts of apple sauce which were force-fed at family meals and pushed on unsuspecting guests. He joked that a frequent query whenever anybody came over was, "Would you like some applesauce?"

At least we were having some chuckles over our differing life-styles and the discourse rarely became dangerously overheated. He was a shop-by-mail advocate and had every Sears catalogue print-ed. I was his gift of modern living, which meant cruising down the aisles of an indoor mall on a Sunday afternoon and stopping at a kiosk for coffee and scones. His way of doing things was cheaper and less fattening. I told him I simply had to be me. He informed me that the "me" I thought I had to be was a roadmap to future poverty. I saw his point and began being me less extravagantly.

I knew my instincts were being bent into a more tolerant at-titude, but becoming a true country wife could take years, and how much slack did I have? At least he got rid of the goats before we traded wedding vows. I will never in my life feel that milking a goat is more fun than shopping.

There were hints that up-to-date culture began permeating our time capsule of a neighborhood of double-wide mobile homes, two hundred-year-old stone cottages and former one-room school-houses. Historic structures were being transformed into small busi-ness emporiums with government grants. Our township was given fifty thousand dollars to loan to an entrepreneur with a plan to draw business into a decrepit area. One guy turned an old caboose into a deli and stocked it with the latest delicacies that upscale city types preferred. These New York City people were now buying up property in the sticks for vacation houses. It was an interesting idea, but the caboose deli bombed anyway. It seemed as though there weren't enough locals who appreciated motif-driven eateries with menus full of veggie wraps and heart-healthy entrees.

Modernity arrived anyway. Huge satellite dishes that had tak-en up entire front yards were now being replaced with small Direct TV® receivers. Wives not only had to have microwave ovens—they began adapting old recipes for pork loins or mutton stews to in-clude kiwi fruit and tofu. These trends gave me some hope that I wasn't totally out of line when I pleaded for a dishwasher. I lost that case because our kitchen really didn't have the space for another inch of convenience.

However, when it came to dressing like a city person versus dressing like a resident of a village in the hills, I tried to stand firm. At first I didn't care that our entire township had one traffic light and the most frequented retail establishment was the convenience store section of one of the Stewart's chain of gas stations. My husband loved commenting about these amenities: He asked me, "Do you know where young fellows take their girls on a night out on the town here?"

"I can't even begin to guess—to the bowling alley near Peter's Supermarket?"

"No. They dress up with clean underwear and head for one of the booths at Stewart's, where they sit opposite each other over a Formica table bolted to the floor to enjoy a dinner of prepared sandwiches, chips and cans of beer!"

"Well, at least the place is centrally located—right across the road from that boarded up bistro and kitty-corner from Gary's Auto Parts. Also, they don't have to worry about where to park the motorcycle."

"And what do they call the intersection with the traffic light?"

"I don't know—they have the Great White Way in Times Square. How about the Great Ice Cream Way to commemorate both the Dairy Queen and the two convenience stores?"

"Are you making fun of Greater Metropolitan Kerhonkson?"

"It's a wonderful place to meet people who carry weapons and go there to discuss the weather."

"You know, you're right—they are always talking about the weather."

"Sure. When I filled up my tank yesterday, I got an earful of the possible rainstorm on the radar. Two inches cause the creeks to flood and they have to close the road—the only road."

"That's why you should wear your rain parka instead of that fancy knit outfit. What happens to it when you get it wet?"

"I give up—you win again. You're slowly but surely converting me from upscale to down home. But don't expect me to do any canning or crocheting."

As time passed, I had to make the leap from one culture to another. I gave up the idea of shopping at places like Saks and Neiman Marcus in favor of driving the twenty-five miles to the nearest decent mall, which was the only mall within the entire county. I could have done a bit of my clothes shopping at the well-known Village of Woodstock, but my desires didn't run to the tastes of the sixties, which is where the Woodstock generation continued to languish, frozen in time. That town was a place where anyone could purchase incense or even a bong without having to search very long. I went there anyway because it was a good place to load up on inexpensive necklaces with fetish designs.

My new favorites had become The Gap and Old Navy. I allowed my collection of practical dresses to remain squashed behind my blue jeans and cotton shirts. The only time this situation annoyed me was when we ventured into Manhattan once a month to see a play or visit a museum. I couldn't make fashion statements any longer, so I settled for store specials from Filene's or J. C. Penney. However, I did tend to slouch a bit in my seat whenever we sat in the elegant auditorium of a New York City theatre to give myself the feeling that nobody would notice my lesser state of posh. Since we walked miles from our favorite Manhattan parking lot to save cab fare and get some exercise, I wore my finest sneakers. Although my slacks outfits were trendy and tended to minimize the impact of flat shoes, it still bothered me. The worst part was when I had to use the ladies' room and keep my eyes averted from the fashion queens in line bedecked with jewelry, gowns and spiked Jimmy Choo heels.

Just when I thought I would sink into the doldrums, I picked my way out of a negative mindset—I started to think about our next trip and fantasized that maybe we could escape to, I mean visit, some of those places I used to salivate about. I couldn't help it, but a smile started to creep across my face and a happy thought about good times ahead interrupted my pissy mood. If I wasn't careful, I'd start beaming. Well, I had the antidote for that—all I had to do was get up off my sofa and telephone the kids. Maybe their tsouras[8] would give me something to fret about after all. Just as I was ready to consult my telephone pad because it had been so long since I'd checked in with the offspring, the fairy godmother came to call. Before I could move a muscle, my mate walked into the room with a sly look on his face. I could tell he was going to elicit some new surprise, and he did.

"Let's go to Ireland."

"Where, my love, did that come from? What travel brochures have you been reading?"

He proceeded to poke a volume of Fodor's right in my face. What could I say or do? I was about to be goaded into living a piece of the life I had always dreamed of. Now what was still on the table that I could complain about? I gave him a luscious kiss and excused myself. Running out the back door, I made for the side lawn where I thought I had spotted a four leaf clover amid the weeds just the other day. Sometimes it was frustrating living so far away from neighbors, because who could I run and brag to at a moment's notice? I understood why little kids often made up phantom playmates. "So what if I'm hyped up and superstitious and a little bit nuts!" I exclaimed to the dryad in the woods. "I'm going to Europe and I didn't even have to nag him—he must really love me!"

As the reality of my good fortune hit home, I began to jump up and down excitedly on the grass I had planted and tended so carefully. I must have been acting like a crazy twelve-year old because The Dog was so startled she dropped the dead ground squirrel she had been saving for her lunch.

Chapter 26
HANDLING HAPPINESS WITH A MINIMUM OF DISCOMFORT

I had never been able to save enough money to travel outside of the United States. Well, I should correct that statement. I had never been able to plan any leisure activity that took place more than six weeks in the future. Now I was being given the opportunity to enjoy another continent. What luck! Well, I probably did deserve it by then.

Only one week before my husband's happy announcement, he had given me another one of his verbal poundings about my tendency to buy gadgets and household items we didn't need. We ended up with a truce that involved my returning six plush towels to J. C. Penney. Just as I was in the process of deciding to take one less bath each week, he must have been adjusting to my display of obedience. Maybe he felt he had been too tough on me and that it was now time to show me a different side of him—his capacity for largesse.

"We're going to Ireland as soon as I figure out which dates will work." He had made the decision without my input and had readied himself for my astonishment.

"What? You just gave me the lecture about saving money! Now, you want to travel to Ireland? Wow! I can't believe you said that! I think I love it! But wait a minute—I don't even have a passport."

"Yes, I know you've been a prisoner of the USA all your life, but they do have a passport office located in Kingston. You could actually go there and apply. It will cost about forty-five dollars. You have to go against your grain and do it ahead of time. I realize that will be difficult, but you can do it."

"I love your confidence in me. What would I do without the way you lead an experienced lawyer around by the nose? I'd fall on my head if you hadn't taught me how to place the flat part of my feet on the ground."

"Just go there right away, OK?" I'll give you directions. You pay the forty-five dollars—I'll pay for the trip."

"Such a deal. You came along just when I thought I would die from continental confinement. Can we go to London too?"

"I've been to London. I haven't been to Ireland."

"I'll see Dublin before I see Buckingham Palace?"

I have a picture book of famous London places. It's on a shelf in my office."

"Now I know what my mother meant when she said 'money talks'. I think I hear her calling now—she's shouting to me: "Take the trip to Ireland, Dummy!"

"I think we should plan the itinerary right now. You can do it—you're good at finding great deals on air fares and hotels and little tourist things. Go girl—I'll show you how to have a good time!"

"Without some new clothes, huh?"

"You have enough clothes."

"I'm a woman. Women need different looks. You don't have that requirement. Why is it when I look in your closet I see hanger after hanger after hanger of beige sport shirts, meticulously hung, and then perfectly pressed shorts and slacks in assorted colors of khaki, olive, light brown, dark brown, shit brown, butternut, taupe and military green? Don't you get bored?"

"I don't think real men should wear flowers or shirts with silly words on them—real men should look like General MacArthur when they're dressed up and like that bluegrass singer, Bill Monroe, when they're casual."

"I think Bill Monroe has been to London, but I'll stop being picky. You can wear what you like. But when we go to certain places, maybe don't stand too close to me if I'm dressed up."

"What's wrong with me and who are you trying to impress?"

"There's nothing wrong with you, but you will never, I mean, never, pick up a magazine for men, such as Esquire, or even Playboy. They have ads for smart outfits for guys."

"You're wrong about Playboy. I pick it up first thing when I go to the barber shop."

"You must skip over the men's ads for fashion."

"I know what's important in life. I've never gotten excited over a tie or even a cravat, but a naked woman wearing a see-through scarf? I have a right to my priorities."

"Are all men like you?"

"I don't interview all men. I suspect that Playboy's circulation is pretty healthy. In our county seat the one haberdasher had to go out of business and stores like Gander Mountain came in. What does that tell you?"

"It tells me that I came a long way from Chicago."

"You did. Now listen up! I want you to leave me and my wardrobe out of it. We're going to Ireland and we'll be doing some pub crawling. I hear it's dark in the pubs, so who cares what I wear as long as I'm wearing something. Don't get your nose out of joint with irrelevant wardrobe issues. We're packing light. Get the passport. Do some research. Oh, and don't forget—I'm a hot guy and hot guys don't need fancy clothes or shirts that look like a Floridian jungle."

"How come you build up your hillbilly image so carefully and then your macho image is tarnished when you take out your ironing board?"

"I like smooth collars and smooth creases on my pants."

"I like it when somebody else does the ironing."

"The discussion is over."

"I'll go to the passport office tomorrow."

As usual, we agreed to agree and I was out of logic and rhetoric for the moment. I had to admit that my loving husband had some good points, some positive feedback, some helpful criticism, and some well-placed zingers. My finances were a mess when he took me on and now I was beginning to accumulate some mutual fund investments, savings account balances and Keogh plan portfolios. I had always known how the tax strategies worked, but had blamed my poor decision-making on my upbringing. Like the proverbial light bulb, I needed to change. Oh well, he saw something in me that kept him hoping. What did it matter anyway? We were having fun.

I went upstairs to my small home office and began to type out some travel ideas on my computer. The Internet hadn't gotten to Kerhonkson yet, but I could sure word process and tax calculate. Then I remembered that I was way ahead of my honey when it came to use of the computer. He was using his daughter's discarded electronic typewriter to write letters and memos to himself. That was my ace up my sleeve. I could outwit him with technology. Again, was I ever wrong about that beige-shirted, plain outfitted bumpkin I thought I had married! The real competition was about to begin.

Chapter 27
THE CLANDESTINE EMERGENCE OF THE GURU

I was in the mood for feeling superior. I had just installed my professional tax preparation software for the year 2000. The millennium had come and gone and nobody had sabotaged our nation or the mailbox in front of our house. I had bought a new Gateway desktop computer with Windows® 98 and everything else I needed programwise had been installed and ready to run. Too bad my husband was such a clod when it came to adapting to high tech. I tried every cajoling tactic I knew, including offering special sexual favors, to tempt him to let me show him how to use a computer. He had to be dragged upstairs to my desk when I insisted he look at my brilliant setup. My efforts had zero effect. He balked, as always, his eyes rolling at me in that convincing manner of his that broadcast: "Don't bother me again with this rot."

Then I tried a more delicate approach. "Why don't you just watch me, while I press the two "on" buttons, and then you'll see how much fun it is!" That suggestion didn't even get me the roll of his eyes. I wondered if I was acting like a woman acts when she thinks she knows more than a man, and then I received his gut level response. Instead of slinking off to his quarters downstairs, he stood face to face with me and made an important declaration: "Leave me alone. I don't need a computer! I will <u>never</u> touch a computer! And that's final!!!!"

Although my offers were rebuffed again, I did not give up all hope. I figured the winds would change one day, just as they had done for Mary Poppins. I heard him descend the narrow staircase and make for his antique private office with his walnut desk and chair from the thirties. That room was a piece of history. On the upper walls hung arrows and bows from another life. Plaques commemorating his mastery in competition pistol shooting were nailed up wherever something else wasn't. Trophies were placed in designated spaces on shelves and a few yellowed favorite cartoons cut out from newspapers were stuck on a cork bulletin board, along with thumb tacked reminders of things to do. An old swaying metal bookcase crammed with his reference books from the days when he worked at home stood precariously in one corner, while his reloading equipment was bolted to the top surface of the only recent acquisition in the room—a custom-made workbench. It was my belief that his carpenter friend had gathered the materials for the workbench from rejected two by fours and sawed off lumber odds and ends from the local Home Depot.

I had followed him downstairs as he got back to work. The door was open and I watched his moves as he retrieved a heavy electronic typewriter that his daughter had discarded several years ago in order to step up to the age of computer technology. First he carefully placed it on his ancient desk, and then he fondled it as he prepared to transact business according to time-tested methods. He seemed to worship that Pre-Columbian clicking monster and did letters, memos and statements on it, using a memory floppy disk system which I never understood.

"How do you find your form letters on that thing?" I asked.

"I label the disks and then I know which one I need, like one of them is when I want to order replacement parts for the snowplow or some other equipment."

"Oh, then you file the disks, like under "S," for snowplow?"

"No, under "FL," for form letters."

"I suppose you file the instructional paperwork for the electronic typewriter under "O" for obsolete?"

"You can leave me alone, now."

"I'm going."

As I digested his abrupt dismissal, I continued to feel superior, but not quite as much as earlier in the day.

We had occasionally engaged in a few conversations about old-timers who disdained modern conveniences. Peg's neighbor, who lived down the road from her, still used a washtub. Lots of women hung up their clothes to line-dry them, but they all had the same excuse: "The clothes come out much fresher and cleaner." I swore by clothes dryers where the laundry was protected from inclement weather. In our household nobody had to worry about some exuberant animal that got the urge to grab a sheet and drag it along the ground with its teeth. It was true that some people hated spending money on new-fangled gadgets, but I had concluded that this wasn't an issue of affordability. I sensed that a few of our old-fashioned neighbors had tons of money—most likely stuffed into canisters, shoved under mattresses and buried in chests hidden in pits somewhere in the yard. I kidded my set-in-his-ways old fogy of a mate that he was almost as bad as his friend, Alvin.

"What's wrong with Alvin?" he asked.

"Alvin types letters that sound like he's never emerged from the forties and on an old Underwood manual typewriter. I know when a mailed envelope is from him, because all the r's and the e's are out of line."

"Leave the guy alone if he's happy living in the past."

"I don't mind him—he gives me something to joke about. But you, with your stubborn insistence on old ways of doing things, like trying to listen to those scratchy '78 RPM' records when you can get CD's now—you're smarter than that."

"I bought you a foot spa—a medical miracle—and it's still in the goat shed, where you store that fancy bike you never use."

"OK, go hang out in your creaky office. Maybe I'll get the camera and a pitchfork and take a picture of you wearing your bib overalls."

"I threw those out."

I walked away because he wanted to be alone in his hideaway. Muttering, "Let him keep his precious space to himself," I gave up trying to be of service. That office of his had begun to take on the aura of the throne room of a monarch, since I had gotten the impression that I needed an invitation to enter it. I wasn't permitted to open the drawers of the ancient desk without his OK because he didn't trust me not to filch his special pens or his meticulously sharpened scissors. Those drawers usually stuck anyway. In all fairness, I did understand the reason for his protective attitude. It seems that when his kids were small they used a small portion of the room as a play center and had been trained that the big desk was off limits. I believe I represented, at least in his mind, a member of a class of frivolous intruders that had to be watched at all costs.

My office was upstairs, but occasionally, even when I was hard at work, I could hear him uttering diatribes when something did not go his way. In modern language, every so often he freaked out. It seemed sensible on my part to stop trying to be helpful.

Shortly after his total denial of my assistance under any condition known to man, I began to re-examine my own organizational shortcomings. "Let's see," I would think to myself, "where did I put that outline I prepared for that new client matter? I know I have it in 'My Documents,' but where the 'h- is it in 'My Documents?' Under the new client's last name? But I can't remember that guy's last name—right now he's only 'Joe.' I know I've got his phone number somewhere—and then there's the legal file I put together—that's somewhere on the floor here...." Eventually, I had to call Joe's referring friend to get the man's last name, which led to my renewed search for where I might have lodged the outline on the computer. Actually, I had to redo it from scratch because I hadn't titled the file under the fellow's last name or his first name. This revelation bothered me. "Maybe, just maybe," I admitted to myself, "maybe my husband's filing system isn't all that bad." I amended my prejudicial conclusion about him and considered the possibility that he might not be this egotistical sputtering monster.

A few days later, while I was sitting in my upstairs office, totally reorganizing my new software disks and completely immersed in my own technological morass, suddenly there came a monstrous barrage of obscenities from downstairs.

"G-d D——- M————f—g S————B——h!!!!!![9] This was repeated several times. The foul expression was loud enough to reverberate throughout the house and make its way up the stairwell. I didn't know if he had broken a finger or screwed up his ammunition reloading press—that weird-looking contraption that resembled a giant meat grinder. Could that be the problem? I ran downstairs to check. His office door was closed. I had heard it slam bang shut with a fury that shook most of the foundation.

"**<u>Don't come in here</u>**!!!!!" He really meant it.

The man I loved was in a steaming frenzy. When he got like that I often took to running outside over to the goat shed to search for one of my trowels. Maybe I could dig up something and find an old Indian relic. They were supposed to be buried all around us. On this occasion, however, I stayed put in the house because through his closed office door I heard banging around and stomping. It sounded like he was smashing something metallic. I hoped it wasn't the window air conditioner or even worse, the precariously assembled old metal bookcase. He must have heard me skulking outside the door because he screamed:

"Stay away! Everything's all right!"

"Gee," I thought, "everything's all right!" Maybe he had a problem with the shelving after all—I had seen it tippy and always wondered how it held its ground. I would never in a million years cross that picket line to overrule his orders. It was infinitely safer, I reasoned, to merely become aggravated with worry and even risk a mild case of stomach ulcers. I went back upstairs and dove into bed, pulling the covers over my head. In a little while he came upstairs and saw me huddling like a waif. "I'm sorry I screamed and scared you," he said in his most apologetic pleading voice. But, please, I don't——"

"I know," I cut him off; "you don't want to talk about it, right?"

"Smart-ass!!" He went downstairs again.

The following day he spent many hours shut up in his castle in that room, totally incommunicado. He emerged for meals and seemed cheery. I thought about some of our nation's great scientists and inventors and how they would forget to eat when they were onto something huge. I didn't think he was secretly ordering a fur coat for me or arranging for a safari for the end of the summer. It had to be something he was immensely worried about. I knew all his moves. He wasn't going through male menopause, although he should have, or suffering middle-aged anxiety syndrome either because he was already too old for that nonsense.

The next few days were uneventful. We had a small flood in the cellar and the dog had a close encounter with a porcupine. I took her to the vet and paid $300 to get her fixed up. There was a head-on collision of two pick-up trucks on our road in front of the house. Our neighbor's home had been ransacked by burglars. The usual. Then in the afternoon of the third day a UPS truck rolled up our driveway. Dirk, the driver, was delivering four interesting boxes. They weren't for me. I wanted to peek, but the boxes had been hastily signed for by my inscrutable husband—obviously a man with some major secret. He must have seen the brown truck and had planted himself by the back door. The boxes were quickly suctioned into his private chamber. I stood near the closed door and could hear the zip of his box cutter and that familiar popping sound when corrugated cardboard yields its contents. Seals were being breached. Again I retreated.

I called one of my friends and chatted for awhile. I told her my husband had slipped a screw or two and might be building a bomb or maybe just a small bear trap. There had been some suspicious scat along the road behind the house. That was a distinct possibility. He would definitely have gone out of his way not to alarm me.

This mysterious activity went on for two more days. Then I was finally let in on the surprise. He met me in bed one night and asked if I was sleeping.

"How could I be sleeping? I'm answering your question about whether I'm sleeping!"

"Well, I have a surprise. You'll like it. Come downstairs."

"OK," I said, friendly—like. "I'm coming." I groped for my eyeglasses, put them on and followed him. He led me into his secret hideaway—the office where he had been holding court for a week. I looked at his desk and it all came together, like all the clues had been there for me to discover.

"You bought a desktop computer. And a printer. Oh, and there's the tower, yes, and wow, some nice speakers, and, what else? Oh, wow, a scanner also? I don't even have a scanner! Well, what happened to the electronic typewriter?"

"Oh, the piece that held the memory disk broke and nobody had the parts to replace it any more."

"So, this is what was going on? You didn't even ask me to help—I could have shown you how to print out an envelope. It took me six months to learn that trick. What word processing program did you get?

"Word®."

"Good."

He looked more than a tad sheepish, but mere words from him were unnecessary. The guilty expression in his eyes said it all. Still, there had to be some cordial follow-up from the bottom of his heart, and, da da! It arrived. He spoke with the syrupy tone of a recovering wife abuser.

"I'm able to do most stuff I need—oh, by the way, I ordered an Internet dial-up connection. You'll be able to use it too."

"That's great. Thanks. So what was the banging noise? What was smashed?"

"I had no further use for the electronic typewriter."

"I see."

"I got angry."

"No kidding?"

"I know you offered to help me learn the computer, but I spent some time reading the instructions and I didn't want to bother you when you seemed busy. Is your offer for sexual favors still open?"

"Well, I don't know. I might have a slight case of ulcers."

"Oh come on—you're just teasing me—oh, I have to ask you one thing—when I go 'Control Alt Delete' and the window comes up asking me about shutting down the task, can I tell them, 'No', I don't want to send an error report?"

My mouth dropped open. That sneak. He had caught up to my skill level in less than two weeks. Well, I reasoned, he still probably couldn't input a tax return, so I guess I can relax.

My temporary balloon of superiority may be temporarily deflated, but I'm certain it will return another day.

Chapter 28
ARE THE STARS OUT TONIGHT?

One evening in late October I noticed that the part of Ulster County where we lived was all aglow. No lights of some small city or alien spying space ships were responsible, nor was the Creator coming to our house for a second shot at our souls. I was pretty certain I had pinpointed a rare night for seeing the stars that Galileo always swore were hanging around. Uncertainty lingered in my mind because when I stood on the driveway where the viewing was possible, the canopy of trees was so thick that it obscured most of the sky. But there was one little place where I could look up and see the constellations. It was right in the intersection of the uphill stretch of the blacktopped roadway and the "T" that ran perpendicular to the run-up. That was the steepest place on the roadway—the pinnacle, so to speak, the spot where my husband had slipped on a bucket of calcium chloride one icy afternoon and cracked several ribs—the area where I could usually feel my galoshes slide around and out from under me as I attempted to de-ice the area. That intersection was simply too wide for a normal person to cross safely in slippery conditions. I guess the tree canopy worried about that dangerous spot also, because none of the lower limbs dared to grow too close to it.

I consulted my husband, who, among his many other achievements, was also a professed weather expert. Correction: he acted like a weather expert. He refused to watch the Weather Channel ever because he did not wish to waste his valuable eyesight time checking the conditions in Texas or maybe Idaho, since we didn't have any property there. His insights on the weather were profound but simple:

"Always dress for anything that may occur."

My insights on the weather were not profound. I believed in umbrellas and he didn't. I worried about getting my hair wet and he worried about having hair. I worshipped weather forecasts printed in newspapers and he pointed out to me that they were usually misleading. I trusted the predictions of the guy who worked at the local gas station and he didn't even trust the warnings of NOAA. He habitually brought his good rain parka with him every time he left the house, no matter which season we were having or what the outside situation was—warm or cold, wet or dry, humid or arid, or light or dark. "The weather outside will fluctuate," he uttered. He would be prepared.

I had an inspired thought that evening and ventured an astronomical query: "Dear, it's unusually clear out—not a cloud in sight. Did you see all the stars lighting up the sky tonite?"

"Nope."

"Don't you ever look up? We have such wonderful star-gazing conditions, you know."

"I look up when I have to."

"Uh huh. Well, I thought I was just now observing the Milky Way up there—I never saw it really during most of my life in Chicago."

"I knew there was one more thing I hated about Chicago."

"We're away from any big city here—almost in the mountains—wow—it's like we could be an observatory and see constellations—doesn't that excite you?"

"I think you know what excites me."

I said nothing further, realizing that a one-track mind is what it is—a set of wheels that can never be derailed prior to death, and possibly beyond. I've never figured out how that type of mind did any deep probative thinking, but I accepted that it was all part of the scheme of things. The stern look on his face indicated that he was about to say something else, so I stood at attention.

"You left your damned work papers in the bathroom—I put them on your chair in your office."

"Oh, thanks. I was so busy, so I was trying to make good use of my free time."

"In the bathroom? You draft documents while you're——"

"Stop—don't make me feel foolish. I had a deadline and I met it and got all sorts of things accomplished!"

"Gee, I wish I could get paid while I dealt with bodily functions!"

"I think you should shut up about my work habits."

"OK, I won't make any more comments about that dead printer that's been sitting on your floor since we got married and you moved your stuff in here. Are you keeping it until it rises from the ashes and talks to you? Maybe spits out a printed piece of paper that it was dying to eject in its last moments? Should we hold our breath in case that piece of hardware manages to run without being plugged in or having its nice little button turned on? It could make a good news story if it woke up, considering what the local paper prints lately."

"I lost you somewhere. You're razzing me about things I haven't disposed of, but I'm not sure about your philosophy—you left me back at the toilet—where I was reconsidering my document drafting experience."

"Maybe you'll take the dead printer to the dump tomorrow?"

"Maybe I'll take you with me when we go there."

"Let's be friends."

"OK, here's my friendly invite: wouldn't you love to go outside with me on this lovely night?"

"I'm still cleaning up after you. You left the pots for me. Oh, remember that fabulous vegetable beef soup you used to make when we first got married? Gosh I loved that soup. When are you going to stir and maybe find the utensil that stirs? I'll even cut up the vegetables for you!"

"You're talking soup and I'm feeling starry-eyed. I need a celestial break from the confines of our love nest. Tonight's the night for going outside and making like an astronomer. I guess you're not coming."

"No comment."

"Love ya," I tossed back at him as I grabbed the rain parka he had purchased for me. I had no plans to wear it, since there wasn't a cloud in the sky. I hated pandering.

Muttering to myself, I could hear my thoughts as though I were speaking them aloud, so I worked on my inflection: "He has to bring up an irrelevant, disproportionate, unimportant, unnecessary, nagging and needling point, which has little effect on my well-being. Why does he do that?" I could hear his answer in my head! "Do what?" He could be counted on to chirp back with some annoying one-liner. I thought up a reply to him which could equalize the dialogue: "Oh, why don't you bug me a little!" There! I can re-chirp with assertiveness. Then he would continue the bird-like dialogue: "You're so easy to bug—you have so many lapses of perfection." I just couldn't stop my running the tape—our imagined conversation—even when we were a couple of hundred yards apart. I guess I enjoyed it as a private little game.

I had wished to change the words of Elizabeth Barrett Browning's poem that began, "How do I love thee?" to "Why do I love thee?" My second line would recite words to the effect that I loved him because...., uh because.... then, as my hurt feelings took over, I postponed completing my version of the poem. Why wouldn't he share certain experiences with me? Was this the battle of the sexes that nobody ever won? He used to be my hero—the guy in the comic book who always saved the girl. And he had actually worked like a comic book artist in the days when he toiled for a living! He kept saying that his specialty was drawing "funny little men with big noses." Wait a minute, why didn't he say that he drew "funny little women?" Or if he did draw funny little women, why did he leave the term "women" out of his oft-repeated punch line? Do I have to face the fact that even in his financially productive days before we got married he was a sexist borderline cynic? And even if he's still a sexist borderline cynic, what does that have to do with watching a bunch of stars?

I realized it was silly to take the parka. I went back into the house for more wisdom. He was in a talkative mood.

"Can't decide whether it's wet or dry, huh? Try feeling the top of your head."

"You're going out of your way to bug me for some reason tonight. I could point out some of your faults."

"I don't have any faults. The last fault I had—I got rid of it—was incorrectly mixing the loads of laundry. No more light pink handkerchiefs for me!"

"Ah yes, the former artist and his failure to discern that new red knit shirts from the boys' department of Jamesway aren't always colorfast."

"You see, I still need you for something."

"I'm going outside to look at the stars without my outer garment. It's about 78 degrees."

"Where outside?"

"The upper driveway—that place where I can see beyond the trees."

"I hate to spoil your party, but you really can't see much from any part of the driveway—you should climb up the hill behind the house where they put the satellite dish. That's the place to go."

"At night—it's scary out there—it's pitch dark and things lurk in the night—upsetting things!"

"Are you reading too many vampire stories? What's up there?"

"Wild things."

"Gee, I knew we should have strung up those cutesy-poo lanterns which would have required running electric wires all the way to the orchard—let's see—we could have lit the place up for only a few thousand dollars."

"Stop it! I'll take the flashlight! I get it! I get it!"

"Have fun. Do you remember where the big flashlight is?"

"Sure. Where is it?"

"Look in front of you—right there on the shelf where it has been for the last five years."

"That's an awfully heavy flashlight. It looks more like a beacon that a lighthouse keeper might use."

"Maybe you'd rather fall on your knee and break a kneecap. Then you'll preserve your dainty little hand muscle."

"I'll take your overgrown flashlight."

I didn't want to go up that hill—flashlight or no flashlight. There were scary animals up there—deer, possums, rats, maybe a black bear and her cub, feral cats, unleashed dogs from the neighborhood, who knows? "Hell", I reasoned, I'm not going up there alone!" My declaration being promulgated, I decided to gaze skyward from that one place on the driveway where the canopy opened—the Big 'T.' Yaaah!

I positioned myself lying on my back on the gritty blacktop to acquire the optimum line of sight. Cranking up my neck to gaze toward the recognizable constellations, which I was certain to recognize, I felt a balky neck muscle telling me: "Don't hold your neck up like that." Well, I listen to my muscles a lot because they warn me when I'm about to go over the edge. I solved the problem by running back into the house to grab my yoga mat and a small head cushion. Since I never did yoga, it seemed like a good alternative use. The scientifically challenged skeptic was in the living room, giving rapt attention to the History Channel on cable TV. Some people can never stop living in the past.

I laid the foam mat right in the "T" of the driveway, where I thought I'd get the best viewing. Lying down on it was no small feat. It didn't feel as comfortable atop the hard blacktop as if I were lying on a cushy rug or even the softer part of the lawn. Groaning and moaning I finally stretched out. Wow, what a breathless sight! The Milky Way, thick as, uh, milk, I guess, wound around the heavens against a backdrop of thousands of stars. I could get hypnotized by such a sight. I finally relaxed and prayed the mosquitoes weren't astronomically inclined. Hopefully they had gone into hibernation wherever mosquitoes hibernate.

Suddenly a vehicle came powering up the driveway. Oh God, with our having no exterior lighting, the driver couldn't see me stretched out on the road in a million years! I had two or three seconds to jump up and ditch the 'T'. Talk about balky muscles! I couldn't do it! In panic I rolled myself over to where the edge of the ravine drops down to the lower forest floor. Thank goodness for lots of trees! I rolled out of the way just as the red pickup made the turn and stopped by the back door. Saved by an adrenalin rush and a desire not to be crushed! Unfortunately, I was now unable to rise to my feet because a low branch had caught on my jeans. It was tickling my behind, or something was tickling my behind.

"Help me up, please," I called to the tall male person who had just emerged from the pickup.

"Who's there? Oh, you! What are you doing lying over there?"

The man was Jim, our down the road neighbor and one of my husband's shooting buddies.

"I just live here," I said. "I was star-gazing on the driveway."

"Oh. I didn't know you were star-gazing on the driveway." Jim walked over to me and assisted while I disentangled the branch from my undies.

"Jim, what brings you to our digs?"

"Well, the wife just brewed up the most amazing vegetable beef soup. She got the recipe from you—don't you remember? She made so much of it I thought it would be nice to bring some for you guys. I hear that you're so busy working all the time—you probably haven't gotten around to cooking much."

"Oh, oh. I'm going to get in trouble."

"Why?"

"A couple of reasons. Nobody here understands me."

"Come on in the house and I'll tell you about the bear that showed up on our porch last night!"

"I can't wait."

My starlit adventure had been interrupted, so I had to be content that I had thoroughly enjoyed my few moments of glorious galaxy gawking. It really galled me that the Milky Way went on without me to keep tabs on it. My blood was still racing from nearly becoming a casualty of a well-meaning country driver bearing soup. I wondered what death by flattening would feel like. I had seen more than my share of Looney Tunes where the hapless bunny rabbit was overtaken by a vehicle and became a rug. As I calmed down I realized that I was still secure in my ample female body. Besides, I was really getting in the mood for some tasty soup as I went back into the house.

The two guys were already in the living room trading stories about bears or guns or ammo or Jim's mother-in-law. A huge container rested atop the counter in the kitchen. The moment had not yet arrived when the three of us could fill our bowls and toast my survival. Quickly I realized that they had forgotten I was there. Men can get as lost in their hobbies as easily as women do.

The social part of the evening ended when Jim excused himself to go home to his family. Left alone with a ton of home-made soup, we jointly speculated on the size of the container on the counter and cooperated by rearranging the entire inside of the refrigerator.

"You're not hungry now, are you? he asked, manipulating my answer away from a yes.

"Oh, of course not, I couldn't eat a thing."

"We'll make a meal out of the soup tomorrow night—I'll buy the croutons and dig up some wine that goes with a hearty soup."

I thought to myself, "Wine with soup? My mother wouldn't have considered wine anywhere or any time unless it was Passover.

As I prepared to drift off to sleep that evening, I realized that I had probably left the yoga mat outside somewhere near the driveway. Geraldine, The Dog, would surely get to it and carry it back to her favorite shredding area. Should I rouse myself and run outside in my nightgown to retrieve it? I didn't think so, because my fluffy bedroom pillow was too too too, uh, just too good a place to rest my neck. Moments before I nodded off, I looked through the picture window and saw a bunch of stars. As Scarlett O'Hara might have remarked, tomorrow was another night.

Chapter 29
WARMING FOR THE STORMING

It's December in beautiful Ulster County. The cows at the Pine Grove Ranch are bedded down and the squirrels are checking around the black walnut trees to see if they missed any goodies. I am reading the newspaper and watching The Weather Channel. I try to convince myself that I love a beautiful blanket of white pristine snow on my rosebushes and other beloved shrubs, but I shriek otherwise.

"Honey, there's six inches of snow on the cypress!"

He looks at me with those eyes at half-mast, meaning I'm about to get a meaningful dose of cynicism. "Snow on the cypress? That sounds like the title of some pop rock tune." He adds a comment under his breath about how much he hates pop rock.

"But I have to rush out there and brush off the branches or the shape will be affected!"

He eyes my own shape and raises his eyelids to three-quarter mast. "I," (he emphasizes his first syllable when the sentence begins with "I,") I make it a point never to interfere with the natural order. A specimen's shape is as God designs."

"Yes, like our front yard grass which we call a lawn? God forbid we should kill all the weeds in it or the onion grass!

"I love my onion grass—don't you kill my onion grass! I love onion soup also. When are you going to make some?"

"Oh, fiddle dee dee."

"I know—Scarlett O'Hara's gentle term for "screw you.""

"I'm going out there to rescue the cypress!"

I shove my flat feet into my boots and throw my winter parka over my flannel pajamas because the cypress hasn't a moment to spare.

It's blizzard time in Paradise Northeast. Our township of Rochester, mecca for the most rough hewn haulers and loggers in Upstate New York, has been referred to by some realtors as the armpit of Ulster County. When the snows come, they spread equal blankets of white on the emerging McMansions and the garbage dumps, providing postcard pretty scenes for viewers from every walk of life.

I secretly enjoy big snows for a secondary reason, however. I can smell the difference in the air. The Dog, Geraldine, is howling more and more every night—she has her own doggie calendar somewhere in her nostrils or wherever she gets her information. My husband has already butchered all the deer we caught this season and now we can call it venison. I'm starting to feel a trifle lonely, however, because the downhill portion of our access road will soon become impassable for any vehicle other than a runaway bulldozer. We pray and hope that the hired snowplowing fellow— the guy with sufficient horsepower to get up the long driveway— has time for us and manages to shovel aside enough of the white stuff so that we might escape when necessary. I always wanted to be snowbound, but that was when I was a foolish young child. Now I'm just a freaked-out cooped up restless older woman. Some veterans of this county would describe me as a whiny city girl.

I've been looking at magazines with titles such as, Florida Design, Southern Living, Palm Beach Estates, etc., and wondering if I will ever get that little house by the beach that I have coveted for a long time. When I say "little," I mean a place that's just big enough for the two of us, no dog or other pet and one guest room for family, but not enough space for more than two of them at a time to hang out with us. Geraldine wouldn't be happy in Florida, for she's a long-haired half-wolf cold weather-loving kind of pooch. If we sell the house, she goes with it. My enjoyment of her antics is one-sided, since she shows little concern for me. I cannot recall any occasion where my efforts to make her life pleasant has been reciprocated. She has never obeyed a single one of my commands nor has she ever once performed for me or made a dutiful fetch of any ball or twig I have ever thrown to her. Heaven knows that I have tried. I mean, do you get, really get, that The Dog doesn't need me, or even worse, doesn't even respect me? So let her be counted as real estate instead of personal property! Now, with that explanation, here's my idea of the ad for our country house in the Houses For Sale section of the Orange County Times-Union:

Lovely Cape Cod, four bedrooms, 1-1/2 baths, kitchen, dining area, living room, 21-1/2 acres of mostly forested wonderland, patrolled by roaming canine who will guard garden plants with a vengeance. Price: Negotiable, or enough so that we can buy in South Florida.

My better half won't let me put that ad in the newspaper. He doesn't want to sell this house because he would miss the hunting too much. I want to sell the house because then I won't have to miss the hunting so much—I will forget about it as soon as I find a nice palm tree to hang my hat on. It doesn't have to be on a beach—it only has to be where a snowflake can't ever land on my nose or eyelashes.

I have concluded by now that I will not miss snow because I've paid my cold weather dues in full—seven winters of grueling and backbreaking labor shoveling steps, essential paths, garage aprons, wood piles and rooftops. And that's only my husband's list! My job is to help him as much as I can, using the auxiliary shovel to gather up whatever snow has been left behind by his greater and more important shovel.

"The small pink plastic shovel is only for the roof," he warns. "Never, I mean, never, use it on the pavement or any concrete anywhere!"

"But it only cost you two bucks ten years ago," you told me. "What's the big deal?"

"I can't replace it. It's not made any longer!" He walks away leaving me to wonder what other roof clearers do when their plastic shovels give out. I never find out.

Another job I am given is to employ the gardening spade to hack away ice wherever required.

"Try to expose the blacktop if you can," he would suggest to me, "but don't kill yourself. Rest frequently and don't lift the shovel if it feels too heavy."

"I'm careful—I'm careful. I know how to do winter! I'm from Chicago! In 1967 we had 26 inches in one weekend!"

"Who shoveled?"

"Uh, we had a young kid that came around."

"Well, do you see any young kids coming now? Let me know because I have two extra shovels."

"I'm your shoveling assistant, honey. And I'm cheaper."

"Oh yeah? I'll be the judge of that."

I wish he would stop reminding me about the cost of my un-reimbursed maintenance. But we always have that silly talk—especially when the temperature drops below twenty degrees. He's right about there being no young kids around, however. Even if there were young kids who lived within a couple of miles of us, any one of them who hadn't taken to flight would have been put upon to do his own family's snow clearing.

✳✳✳

The moment has come for action—it's the winter equinox and the breakfast dishes have been washed and shelved still wet.

"Why do you put dishes away wet? I asked him that only once.

"Have you ever heard of evaporation? It's a process where drops of water are absorbed into the air."

"I always let my dishwasher do that."

"I'm your dishwasher, baby." He lets his hazel-green eyes stare at all of me to prove his point.

He leads the way out of the overheated kitchen into the frigid outside. "OK, woman, are you ready for a good hunk of exercise? Do you feel up to it?" Was he kidding? I wasn't about to make a few phone calls and get a bridge group together.

I give him my sweetest cooperative look, like the fabulous helpmate I have become. The more I perform the more respect I will gain.

In terrible weather we did strive to have fun. We were a team. He played Laurel and I played Hardy. I had dressed with so many layers I resembled a walking ball of yarn with mittens. There was a purpose to that—if I fell anywhere, I would bounce safely. The extreme protection I employed gave me comfort and I answered his call. "I'm ready to roll, lover, one hundred percent! How about a little NASCAR intro? Gentlemen—start your shovels! And there goes the man in the brown fleece jacket and the knee-patch pants—he's off and running!" By the time I finished my intro, he couldn't hear me through his earmuffs.

I had learned the moves by then. Usually, I followed him as he muscled the large plowing shovel forward, making a succession of overlapping four-foot wide sections to serve as a walking path along the two hundred foot length of the driveway that led from the kitchen door to the garage. I thought of him and the way he worked as similar to the famous Alaskan dogsled hero, Balto, the lead dog of the legendary Nome medical rescue. If my husband was now the official lead dog of our shoveling party, I was a team dog, a creature of lesser endurance, figuratively harnessed behind him, having been fed and petted. My task was to widen the path to five feet or more, if possible, which was easier than being on First Shovel. Often we performed this ritual while it was still snowing, because if we allowed too many inches of the stuff to pile up, it would pack down and become dangerously dense and we would be candidates for heart attacks.

My consolation was always the thrill of totaling up all the calories I was no doubt expending performing these cold weather marathons. Since I couldn't actually tally them scientifically, I tallied them mentally by gauging the amount of sweat I accumulated inside my parka. If my sweaters were really drenched, then I gave myself a post-shoveling party of an extra lunch sandwich and whatever dessert I could scrounge up. I never knew exactly how my input of food and output of energy balanced out, but I can guarantee that I never lost any weight in the winter.

Sometimes I engaged in reverie about my suburban Chicago snowstorm experiences. My townhouse had a driveway that could hold about four vehicles, if I ever got three other people to come over, and there was a short path to my front door. I kept my car in the garage. I never even made a phone call to initiate the clearing of snow. My homeowners association dues took care of everything and the hardest thing I had to do was back my car out of the garage on the way to my office without getting stuck in a drift, or hitting the mailbox. When I think of how simple my life was then, I wonder at the same time if my arm muscles would have eventually atrophied from lack of use. Running a vacuum cleaner wasn't quite as exhilarating as those physical pleasures I enjoyed now.

We toiled like heavy maintenance types, except nobody paid us. He reminded me that in Buffalo, New York, people didn't shovel on top of the pile of snow—they made tunnels under it. After the main driveway was done, I looked forward to a solid three hours of ice hacking or holding onto the husband's ladder as he descended from the roof after ridding it of a ton of snow. After each stint, I used to run to the hall mirror to see how red my nose and cheeks had become so I could think of myself as Mrs.Clause or Bozo the Clown.

"Do you wish you were back in Chicago, honey?" He always asked that with a sly suggestion in his voice because he knew I would never say that I was. After a really tough bout of weather he enjoyed getting out of his wet clothes and taking a hot shower. He boasted of spending the whole afternoon making love, but right after the shower he would soon feel the effects of the morning and wind up taking a fairly long nap, leaving me to my own devices. I spent a lot of cold afternoons daydreaming about spring flowering trees, summer flowering lilies and, eventually, tiki bars and white sand beaches.

I never missed my townhouse nor did I long for my single woman's sheltered routine. But I was beginning to feel as though

I had had enough of the snow brigade routine. The question was, had he? So there I was, and, being wedded to an outdoorsman—a gritty fitness addict—and buying into all of his do-it-yourself bravado because I was in love, I made myself happy with intriguing little ideas for a few harmless stunts.

Whenever I became overly restless in the winter, I would begin to search for just the right activity. Sitting on my ergonomic chair before my computer did not seem satisfying for long, although I invented a few new pastimes by playing around with the default drawing program. Why not? I was always brainstorming about how I could indulge my creative instincts, so I had written little verses about longing for tropical breezes. Then I got bolder and drew colorful pictures on the computer using the "Paint" program. I began with strokes revealing stucco houses with Spanish tile roofs and porticos and Moorish windows. Then I graduated and began to design more elaborate Victorian houses. They always included summer landscaping and never included winter scenes. But right then, since I was a shut-in, my only break from the routine seemed to be my confrontation with ten degree weather. After much regression into my memories of a childhood and building snowmen and watching ice sculpture, it soon became a certainty that I would have to engage in some outdoor recreational activity or I would go mad. Would he understand it, or would it only serve to annoy him because he was forever second-guessing my choices?

✵✵✵

I've just dreamed up something new to do after lunch. Our afternoon plans are already having hiccups and I need to be entertained, so I visit the tool shed and prepare for my mischief. Then I return to the house to dress for the occasion. He happens to enter the bedroom as I am clothing myself for my secret romp.

"Why are you putting on those extra wool socks?" he asks. "You hate wool."

"They're not wool—they're look-alikes. They're fake warm socks, but they'll keep my toesies warm when I go sledding."

"You're not, uh, oh no, you're not taking the kids' old sled from the shed and thinking you can go down the hill behind the house, are you? Oh my, I guess you are. Do you know how tough that will be? The ruts are gravel and the snow will not pack down enough for you to have a real track!"

"Yes, they will. I got the big shovel out and scooped a whole layer of extra snow all along the sledding strip and packed it down already. I was thinking of pouring some water on the ruts last night and then it would be icy, but I think that's going a little bit too far, don't you?"

"You're cuckoo."

"I'm bored. I haven't sledded anywhere since I lived near Gompers Park in Chicago."

"You were a small girl then—well, a young girl then—you were a short plump teen-ager. You had a layer of baby fat and a cute face. I remember you that way. If you used a sled, it was not down a hill like ours. The only hills anywhere near Chicago were made out of old garbage. Remember Mount Trashmore in McHenry County? "

"I was a dare-devil then. I'm still overflowing with vim and vigor. I'll be careful."

"You'd better build in a natural stop when you get to the driveway or you'll go right down the ravine and break something."

"Oh, thanks for thinking of my welfare."

"I was thinking of the trees' welfare. You could snap one of the smaller ones."

"There are no smaller ones. They're all a match for me and my sled. I'll be careful."

I went out as planned and stomped over all the packed ruts again to be certain the sled wouldn't be hung up on any underlying gravel while I tobogganed my heart away. I wanted to break a record. At the bottom of the hill, I grabbed some manageable limbs and laid them across the path as a natural stop. The sled would be interrupted gently and I would safely call it a day. As an afterthought I put in a second barrier at the edge of the ravine. I was now ready to take off. Too bad I couldn't capture my own snapshot of my trajectory. I shlepped up to the top of the hill and arranged the length of me on the sled, belly down. Then I thought, "No, I could hurt my head because it would be first—I'll sit on the sled and grab the sides with my hands to hold on." I took off with a mighty push.

"Look out below!!!!!" I was calling to the air around me. Nobody was watching. It was too humdrum a stunt for The Dog or the Man. I was just doing my downhill racing for whichever birds had deigned to hang loose for the winter—chickadees, doves, maybe a blue jay or two. There I went really fast—too fast——too too fast——way too fast!!!! Oh no, I'm going to crash! Ooohhhhh-hh!!!!" The sled hit my first barrier on the driveway and its momentum jolted the runners over it. My failsafe design worked, however, because the sled came to an abrupt halt right at the second barrier next to the drop-off. However, I didn't. I was propelled ahead like a human missile, smacking into a tree halfway down the ravine.

Contrary to published reports by people falling from heights who are headed for something pretty dreary, time didn't stop. At first I did not move an inch. I recall thinking about some daredevil I had once observed—yes—there was something about a cannon. Then, like a bug that narrowly averts death by squashing, I flexed my limbs—thanking the Creator that there were only four of them and not six or eight. My next thought was—did my hair get mussed? My woolly cap had been zapped off halfway down. So much for cheap old hairpins. Finally, after a brief conversation with my ego, I decided it might be a good idea to determine if I was still ambulatory. As I slowly raised myself up by grabbing a slender tree trunk, I did feel something ominous. Thinking I had broken something other than a few saplings, I used that small trunk as a rock climber might use an outcropping by clinging to it for temporary survival. I was better off than a rock climber, however, because I fell where years of unchecked growth had covered all the underlying rocks. Fortunately, my point of descent was yards away from the discarded farm and lawn equipment. Another good stroke of fortune was my ample padding of extra layers of clothing. I let myself gently slide down the rest of the way to the bottom. I had lost a glove and skinned my right hand and my left arm didn't feel like it was screwed on right. I tried to flex it. It was bending correctly, after all, but something was painful. I got up and attempted to walk. I could walk, although haltingly. I tried to call out. "HELP!!!!" The Dog came running over to me and circled around me. She sniffed my pants legs which were encrusted with dirty snow. She sniffed where I always hated she sniffed. What kind of an unnatural act was that! I'm a human—not a sex object for a wild mutt. Then she left and didn't even bother to wag her tail much. I wasn't worth it.

I was able to walk up a gentle path out of the ravine and decided two things: one that I hadn't broken anything important, and two, sledding just wasn't going to do it for me. I entered the house and found a large dressing for my exposed flesh. It did not hurt much. I was still desirous of something exciting. Where was my husband? He could be exciting sometimes. I found out his nap was over because there was no lump in the bed. He must have gone outside.

I found him by the wood pile, heaping fresh split logs smack against the front stairway wall—he was covering up the clinging ivy. I had planted the sprouting vines meticulously. They were the hardy kind that would survive a freeze. My design had worked perfectly. The thick vines decoratively masked the brick sides of the front steps. I planned that feature in order to hide the crumbly mess the old wall had become because the brick hadn't been tuck pointed for one hundred years, if ever.

Despite my aching and disheveled self, I still had some fight left. I pleaded with him, "Please don't cover up my ivy—it took a long time to grow it—think of Wrigley Field. Would you ruin the beautiful ivy growing in center field?"

He stared at me without noticing my bruised condition and thought I was crazy. "This is where the firewood goes. Do you want me to shlep it a half mile? I'm an old man getting older. What kind of selfish person are you?"

"Can't you just put the firewood where there's no ivy?"

"This is where it goes."

"Can I just speak on behalf of a poor unrepresented member of the plant kingdom for a moment? Pretend you're one of these lovely green leaves and this big bad man is going to snuff out your air and stop your chlorophyllization. Wouldn't you beg for mercy?"

We began to tussle. My mind had gone into obsession mode, which is much like going blank, but I was probably the one who hit first. He tried to stop my flailing arm from landing a punch. I didn't follow the rules for wrestlers. Wrestlers don't scream, "Get away from my Ivy!" Finally, he gave up. He was so angry with me he stalked off in a cold-blooded huff. I had won another pyrrhic victory. The ivy got to live and he got to hate me. Now I had to go lick his boots or something. This adamance which I had read about in all the feminist literature didn't get the predicted results with a real macho wood-chopping fanatic. He hadn't read those books. I believe the best word to describe him was implacable. The best word to describe me was miserable. I had been married to him for seven years now and I still had to adjust to his extremely firm personality. There was only one emotion left for me to express with any sincerity—a three-year-old's version of despair. I became a tearful, childish, peevish, crying infant—and was I ever good at it. I ran inside the house and made a bee-line for the lair of the wood stove.

My tears flowed as a leaky faucet as I remained flopped and inert on the living room sofa. For an hour or so I cared more about the welfare of the ivy than myself. The haunting strains from an old Doris Day song containing lyrics with the words "the ivy clings to the vine" rang in my ears. I figured there must have been a technical name for this type of disease, but I didn't know what it was. Out of my utter collapse of rational thought, I made up a new term—floracideaphobia—fear of the death of plants. I stopped wailing as soon as I realized I had a new dictionary entry. It was really a palliative moment. I sprang into maturity and thought about my marriage and my firewood-loving hero. This return to basics required that I get off the sofa. I went to find him, and there he was, nice and clean and just emerging from the shower with a ratty towel about his bottom. In that tiny segment of time between my loss of marbles and my instant recovery, I realized that he was more important than a plant.

I only sniffled a bit as I spoke: "I'm very sorry I gave you a hard time and I apologize. I'll never do that again."

"Do what again?"

"Come between you and your firewood."

"Oh, well, I can heap it somewhere else, but you were really nasty—you were out of control—you were wrong."

"I was?"

"Isn't that what you just said? I thought I heard an apology. Are my ears failing me?"

"Oh yes, but I was very much in control when I ranted and raved. I knew exactly what I was doing when I struck you on your firewood-stacking hand. I wanted to make you stop—I wanted you to obey me."

"Obey you?"

"Yes, like the wedding vow says—love, honor and obey."

"That vow was about something else. It wasn't intended to make us spend more money by forsaking firewood and using the radiators instead of the wood stove. Who pays for the electric and propane bills? I do. Who pays for the heating oil? I do. Who pays for the axe? Not you. Who pays for the—-?"

"I get the point. But I paid for the trowel that dug the holes that held the roots that sprouted the vines that grew the leaves that covered up the brick that adorned the house that the farmer built." I did."

"I lost you somewhere. I think you said you paid for a trowel—that cost about $3.00, tops."

"That's more than you paid for your pink shovel, and, besides, what about my labor?"

"You needed the exercise. I'm tired of this argument. I don't want——"

"To talk about it any more!!!! I finished his sentence—a well-practiced art I had honed. And then I pre-empted his favorite follow-up. "I'm through talking about it!!!" I stayed in his face while he stared.

"You're standing in my way."

"I'm waiting for a kiss."

"I'm not in the mood."

"Just one little one."

I received a tiny peck. The smaller and more indifferent the kiss was, the less he wanted to placate me. Let me tell you, this peck was really small—a token that wouldn't add up to three cents. I guessed that it was all I deserved at the time. This was one more minus on the scorecard of loving, which would require something magnanimous on my part later on. Amends always have to be made in any relationship worth its salt.

✳✳✳

I had had sufficient winter fun for a season. But, as I said, it was December. We needed a winter vacation. My firewood loving ivy-mistreating man of my dreams was not all bad and not all good. He was terrific. He told me he thought we should go to the islands in the Caribbean for a couple of weeks. Would that be OK? Well, sure, I thought. The ivy could go into hibernation and we'd have to spend some money for a really dedicated mutt-sitter, but I thought it was a go. I put away my copy of Florida Design and made a note to buy a copy of Island Living next time I passed a magazine stand.

I didn't have a bad life at all—just an adjustable one—like a seat belt. When he threw the curves at me, I just strapped myself up tighter.

Chapter 30
KILLING ME SOFTLY WHILE DRIVING (OR HIKING)

Before the era of the GPS, we had the era of driving complicated routes by the seat of one's pants. I am skilled at finding my way around. My husband has a perception problem. He doesn't look at obscure landmarks like I do when I'm in the driver's seat. He calculates. Actually, I don't know what he does. When a driver doesn't know whether to turn right or left, because he has come to a choice of turns with no written directions, wouldn't you expect him to guess correctly at least fifty percent of the time? Well he guesses wrong about 75% of the time. I've kept track. And when he misses a turn or a ramp exit or a road sign, he gets over-excited, like the world is going to come to an end. The swearing begins where the trail leaves off.

It's even worse when I'm driving because even though I have a pretty good idea of which way to turn, he doesn't, and he bestows his confusion on me. He yells and carries on and claims I don't know where I'm going because he can't concentrate on where I'm going. "We're lost! I know we're lost! We're nowhere near where we should have turned! Go back to that place five miles back where I knew for sure we were in the right place!"

He wants me to retrace and go all the way back to the parking lot that we had just left so that he could calculate some more. I, however, knew nearly exactly where we were because I knew in which direction we were heading and approximately where the next turn should be. But he's yelling so loud in my ear that I'm risking losing my calm—my emotions are wavering between smugness and fear—I'm smug because I use mental tricks to remember indicators and I'm fearful because he can make me doubt my whole philosophy of life in a screaming sentence or two. If I try to argue or interrupt he closes up his face to prove a point. It's the way he does anger, but it's different with him. I'm afraid if things get too wobbly, he's going to go into his version of a pout. My pouts are mild and female and usually resemble the face one makes with indigestion or cramps. His pouts are demonstrative and ear-splitting. They are similar to the way baseball managers argue with umpires.

My hurt feelings pretty much stay inside me, which makes me want to talk my way out of a bad situation. His hurt feelings don't exist because he is hardly ever wrong. How can a nearly perfect person feel hurt when the other party to the argument has probably made a mistake? I could recount one recent incident when we were looking for the Kaaterskill Falls area near Haines Falls, in Greene County, New York. I was a bit lazy about consulting the map, but I had been there and had confidence I could find it again. He didn't trust me to find it.

"Do you know exactly which route it's on? You seem to be guessing?"

"Of course I do—it's either State Route 23 or 23A—one of them."

"Wait a minute—those roads are not right next to each other! How do you plan to go down the right road?"

"Well, if the road sign says we're heading towards Hunter, then I know we're going on the right road."

"But where do you pick up that road sign? Don't you have to know where to turn before that?"

"Oh, I just follow my instincts. I know approximately where Hunter is."

"Your instincts? Your instincts? It takes time and gas mileage to check out your instincts. I insist you look at the map!"

"OK, it's in the side pocket."

"You've got twenty maps in the side pocket."

"I know, that's why it's easier to just go north on Route 9 until we get to the area near Hunter. What's the big deal? It's in Greene County!"

"You're talking about an entire county and you don't think it's a big deal?"

"OK, I'll pull over to the next gas station."

"I can't stand the way you adlib your driving based on some gut feeling you have. Why don't your gut feelings help you when you ask me the dumbest questions two or three times? You don't pay attention to me when I answer you the first time."

"Oh, I do pay attention, but usually you explain stuff while I'm still working on the previous questions. Your answers don't exactly queue up, you know."

"All right, let's just get to the Falls. Here's a sign—it says we're leaving Greene County, entering Schoharie County. I think we're lost."

"Oh, I know where we are—I'll make a U-turn at the next driveway and we'll find the road. I just passed up one little street— no biggie—I can see the peaks surrounding Hunter Mountain from here."

"You drive me nuts."

"Look!!!! Look!!!!! What's in front of us? The road to Hunter and look again—there's the sign for the road to the Kaaterskill! I knew we were on the right track."

In about fifteen minutes we were passing up the spectacular roadside view of the famous waterfall area—a place where legends of explorers and early settlers were documented in books for tourists. I looked at him to see his expression. He was implacable. I knew that in less than five minutes I would receive a studied apology and retraction of sorts. He was quicker this time.

"I'm sorry I got upset with you. I guess you did know how to find the place."

"No worries. I know that my system for locating places is strange. I think somewhere in my ancestry is one of those geography savants—that person probably had a penchant for reverse logic and it was passed down to me."

"How come you can't seem to find anything in your desk when you need it?"

"That's different—that's cabinet and drawer methodology—lack of conscious attention to where papers get shuffled during paper shuffling. All lawyers have that problem."

"Let's take some pictures."

"OK, but I'm not climbing up those wet rocks! You can do it, but I'm staying put—right here by the off-road scenic area sign."

"You can't even see the upper part of the falls from there."

"I'll see the upper falls when I see your photos."

"Come on—we came all the way out here!"

"Oh, you're such a pest!"

I followed him to the trailhead and watched as he ascended about one hundred feet. I ascended about twenty feet and let myself take a little coffee break. He had good feet. I had bad feet. I was good at finding places. He was bad at trusting how I found places. What a pair we were! But the real test of our differences came when we decided to take a waterfall trip to a remote area of North Carolina. It was a trip where his stamina came head to head with my delicacy. The agenda for that destination further defined one of my critical issues in our aging lives and differing conditioning: Were we once again embarking on a series of trails intended for twenty-somethings or people with iron legs? I could have added a small addendum to whatever description the sweet-sounding brochures contained regarding the hiking, and that was: "Older more sedentary types need not apply."

✳✳✳

I should have read the book he carried. It described in minute detail where each scenic waterfall was located and the degree of difficulty involved in getting to where a person could actually see each scenic waterfall. If I had read the book I would have known that when it said point five eight of a mile as the length of the trail, the incline or decline of the trail mattered more than the long or short of the matter. A downhill trail where huge snarly tree roots and slippery drop-offs occurred was more challenging than a level trail with an even and dry coating of gravel. In my heart I desired a trail for beginners and older women, while he wanted the finest possible scene for an award-winning photograph, no matter what the cost or wear and tear on the muscles. We compromised, as usual, meaning we did it his way.

I'll skip over one particular five-mile uphill rather dull road to an advertised lookout that seemed like an anti-climax when we finally reached the crest. We had already been there and done that. I'll also skip over another place where we met up with foreign-language-speaking friendly couples who had skinny long legs and moved like triatholoners. I stayed back at the pass at that juncture and took photos of sunlit leaves and insects crawling along moss-covered logs, while the rest of them emerged from their dizzying climb with pictures of the best waterfall in the county. OK, so my lack of exercise and short plump physique dictated my hiking decisions. Phooey, I thought to myself as my husband came back down the trail, "Bully for you—I'll outlive you by twenty years!" Well, sometimes I thought like that.

What I won't skip over is the one particular trail to a waterfall area that the book author rated highly. The description made it sound fairly accessible for both of us, so we found the trailhead and parked the car. I began to have a sliver of doubt when an older couple appeared in the parking lot, having just done the loop hike. The woman was shaking her head and seemed to require assistance getting back into their vehicle. I also observed the way she was walking. It was more like limping. Just then another older couple arrived at the parking lot. They got out of their car and I saw that the lady was wearing flip-flops. She spoke to her husband for a moment and they walked over to the hikers' information board and then promptly returned to their car and drove away. I thought that one of the words she uttered was "shopping."

"Maybe we should pause a moment," I whispered.

"She wasn't prepared for this hike and did you see his beer belly? He wasn't either." My husband always sized up the sizes and physiques of strangers. Then he turned to me and said, "You can do it. Just take your time."

So we set off on the gentle downhill slope at the trailhead—
me hesitantly and he eagerly. It was supposed to be two miles long
each way and did not involve really steep uphill or downhill scram-
bling. As we hiked single file, however, the path got more rugged
and I started to have opinions. By now I had become assured that,
while the author of the book was a knowledgeable sort, he had to
be an athletic fellow as well as a noted photographer. He meant
well.

We decided we had to have our tripods. Mine was not collaps-
ible, so my husband, the hiking optimist, helped me tie it up se-
curely to my backpack. His backpack was heavier than mine, containing extra lenses, more equipment and was well, just heavier.
My backpack was heavy enough for me.

I did fine for the first one-eighth of a mile, gingerly stepping
over the worst of the emerged tree roots and avoiding the muddy
gunky spots. The trail meandered as trails do—they wind around
trees and obstacles, but I know in my heart they are designed especially for hapless people to get lost. It's a conspiracy and it ought to
be dealt with out in the open, but life is unfair and so is my genetic
disposition.

We traipsed and then he called out to me, being about three
hundred feet ahead: "How are you doing?"

"I'm managing."

"How's the backpack?"

"It's fine. It's heavy. It's a cross I have to bear."

"OK, let's keep going."

"I'm not complaining."

"I can feel your inner complaints like I was telepathic."

"Stop doing that," I requested.

"Stop complaining silently," he demanded.

We plodded along for another couple of minutes and then his body disappeared. I shouted out: "I can't see you—what happened?"

His head suddenly showed up. "Oh, the trail does go downhill. Watch your step here!"

"Goody." I thought. As though I wasn't going to watch my step unless he announced that I should. Men!

Eventually we got to the waterfall and it was glorious and we did take great pictures, but the author of the book had indeed lied through his teeth. The trail had been rated mildly strenuous. I was ready to check into a clinic from exhaustion. If this was good exercise, then I wanted to try bad exercise, or no exercise.

"Are you satisfied with your shots?" he asked gently.

"Yes, I'll show you my best. Come here and look at the back of my camera!"

He did so and smiled at me and I felt vindicated for having reached the scene and having remembered at least half the camera settings I needed to adjust. "Let's call it a wrap and go back now," I suggested.

"Hurry up, it's almost dusk."

"Wait a minute," I called as he began to walk along a path, "You're going downhill! We have to go uphill!"

"This is the trail. You forgot!"

"No, we got here by going downhill. I remember."

"But then where's the right trail?"

"Not where you're going."

"I'm right. This is the one that's clearly marked! Look over there."

"I think you're wrong. That's an alternate path to something else."

He disagreed, so we went his way and I didn't remember any of the vegetation or pattern of the stones as we descended for about a half mile. I should have clobbered him with my sense of direction, but I wasn't certain myself. It was getting dark. "We're wrong," I said finally. "I know we didn't go uphill at all for the last part of getting to the waterfall—we have to reverse ourselves!"

He scrambled back up to me and looked as apologetic as he knew how. "You're probably right, but when we reach the waterfall again, how are you going to find the right path?"

"The right path will be uphill. Trust me."

We went on in the near darkness. As we reached the water-fall again, which was now barely visible in the dim light, I tried to remember how far I had walked as the path leveled off. I re-membered a rock that had some yellow flowers growing around it, but it would be hard to see now. He had taken out his flashlight. Then he remembered that he carried a head lamp and he gave me the flashlight. No wonder his backpack was so heavy. I used the flashlight successfully and soon found the yellow flowers and then we both saw the uphill path. He trudged along close to me and hugged me because sometimes I was valuable. This was one of those times.

"You're better than I am at directions," he admitted.

"I notice landmarks. Also, it's harder for me to hike, so the scenery goes by me slower. And, by the way, that explains the Theory of Relativity."

"Oh shut up. You already won the debate."

"I don't care about winning—I want to get back to the car and faint for a little while."

We found our way back and the stars were twinkling as we got into the car. "You'd better drive," he said. Then he added, "I love you."

"You do? Enough to go to that pricey Italian restaurant back in town?"

"Yes. That much."

The hike was over and the big question I asked myself was: Had I had enough exercise to justify eating such a big meal? Probably not. I knew the statistics. Thirty-six miles makes one pound of fat. I wondered if hiking along sloping muddy miles meant I could indulge a bit more.

We gorged on a huge and delicious meal and then returned to our rustic cabin. I went to bed and finally fell asleep, still stuffed to the gills, as my mother used to say. Some day I'm going to research the origin of that expression. I really don't believe that fish overeat.

Chapter 31
CONTINUING EDUCATION COURSE ON MARITAL FIGHTS—GLOVES NOT INCLUDED

I remember about three occasions in the last ten years when I seriously wondered if I had made a marital mistake and would have been better off remaining single. My personality and sensitivities have never been what I describe as thick-skinned. There are weaknesses in my relationship resume and flashpoints in my ability to withstand criticism. In other words, I'm probably not cut out to be a CEO or an elected official. I'm definitely not the type to be a union leader or a drill sergeant. Do they even have women drill sergeants? Well, you get my point. I'm soft in the middle.

Our arguments can get pretty zesty, but I'm not about to make a laundry list of what they're about. Just trust me—they usually involve what I refer to as "territory." And that is what I've been beating my chops about here—each of us has fought over our turf and our choices. We've disagreed vigorously about a few areas that are often the subject of fights in the lives of a couple: spending, house cleaning, buying furniture, meal planning, spending, listening to each other, entertainment choices, politics, spending, socializing with friends, sleep habits, health and fitness choices, spending, driving habits, TV watching, and, last but not least, finances.

The most recent fight I remember was over two place mats in our kitchen. Yes, as I've hinted at here and there, it's the little things that can raise the roof. Well, you see, he is a hard-ass about cleaning certain things, while I notice that he misses other things. He's always making popcorn and I always find salt all over the counter when he's finished. But if I miss the place mats, well, get out the scorecard and take note.

✳✳✳

I had come back from the beauty parlor about noon one day, after having dilly-dallied at my computer prior to my leaving the house that morning. I was supposed to have finished cleaning the kitchen before I left. I enter the house and I'm salivating from thinking about how nice my hair looks and how attractive and kiss-able I am. He's coming toward me and not smiling.

"I have a bone to pick with you."

"Oh, oh, what did I do now?"

"It's what you didn't do—you left the kitchen without finishing the breakfast dishes, but the worst part of it was the filth you didn't clean up on the place mats!"

"Oh, I'm sorry; I was in a mad hurry."

"That's not why I'm upset. I'm upset because you don't care at all about me—you think I'll just clean up after you." He is scowling and quite angry.

This issue is not going away. We proceed to have a row that is the type of shouting match that my mother used to fear. At a certain decibel level of screaming she would remind my father that the neighbors could hear. But they lived in an apartment then. We live in a house in Florida with concrete walls where we could kill each other and nobody would find our body parts for days. But I'll spare you the dialogue. You've probably had it if you've been married for awhile.

So please, just imagine about a forty-five minute period at the end of the shouting match where he is sitting on his territorial place on the sofa, while I'm sniffling in my office trying to make sense of something on my computer and not succeeding. The back-and-forth verbal back-biting had proceeded far enough and when you get older, you know you don't have that much time left to redo your personalities. I'll be fast-forwarding over those unfriendly insults and descriptive action words which portray a husband trying to out shout his wife, who is not only a great shouter, but a talking lawyer, to boot. Instead, here's the run-up to the finale:

I put my hands on my hips and calmly state: "You need an anger management course."

"Don't give me psychological bullshit. Anger management is for pussycats. You need to be told off once in awhile."

"It's not bullshit—you caught me by surprise. You know I've been trained how to argue: I've had four different therapists, group encounter sessions, EST, two prior marriages, each with counselling, advice columns up the kazoo, and gab fests over the Internet. What training have you had?"

"I never needed training, not even the toilet kind."

"Well, it's just not fair." I realized I shouldn't have said that last thing—I knew he would come back with his standard response that life wasn't fair.

"You know, life isn't fair. You ought to grow up."

"Thanks. I'll remember that. I want an apology from you for overreacting and then I'll apologize for leaving the dirty place mats."

"I'm not ready to apologize. You apologize."

"OK, I apologize."

"OK, let's forget the whole thing. Just try to remember to clean the place mats when it's your turn."

"Why is it that you make all the rules around here?"

"I said forget it. It's over. No more questions."

"What's over?"

"Everything. Stop talking about it."

"OK, I'm stopping." I sit next to him on the sofa, where he always plants himself on his untouchable cushion—the one I'm not allowed to encroach on. I watch him with tear-stained eyes for a few moments.

He reads the paper as though everything is back to normal. I feel stupid, like I'm a two-year-old who just got bawled out. Like I can't even open my mouth, which is, for me, a pretty difficult feat. What can I say at this point? The judge has pounded the gavel and court is adjourned.

If there is one thing I hate that he does, it's when he tries to shush me. I've never been graceful when people try to shush me. Maybe that's why I like to write so much. The computer lets me type until it runs out of gigs. So I keep upgrading the gigabyte capacity. Humiliation is not easy for me. Besides, he still hasn't complimented my new hairdo. Do I need him to? Do I need approval? You bet I do.

With me it's automatic. After returning from the beauty parlor, an activity which I pursue about every six weeks, out of my mouth comes the same question every single time—"How's my hair?" It's so routine with me I don't even wait for an answer. I just need another human to exchange words with after spending two hours in a salon located next to a retirement community. Do I have to draw a picture of who their patrons are? They're the women in the hair club that I'm about to join. There are more wheelchairs, walkers, canes and nurses in that salon than there are photographs of twenty-year-old models. I've yet to see a single photograph on their wall of a model over age fifty with thinning hair and even one solitary wrinkle. I figure I've got a little time before I face the reality of being called "elderly," but the realization is beginning to hit home. When I leave that place I need a pat on the back more than anything else. Even my judgmental husband says that everyone needs a pat on the back. So why am I getting his cussing instead? I open my mouth and gape at him with the telltale quaver that precedes a talkative wife's attempt at a concise but emotional statement.

"Speak," he says, knowing that I'm trying. I resent the fact that he always has to control the conversation, but that's just the way it is.

I speak. "Everyone needs a pat on the back."

"OK, your hair looks nice. I guess I talked out of turn."

"Yes, it hurt. I forgive you for harboring the grievance and I apologize for being careless about your time."

"Oh, you'll do it again."

"And, of course, you'll occasionally lose your temper again."

"Who me?"

The innocent expression takes over and that's the signal that we have made up and that it's time to let our individual egos hang loose and get back to being in good humor. It's a system which I recommend if anybody can identify with this type of discord.

✻✻✻

I think we'll never patch up all our differences, and even if we did, wouldn't that be rather dull? Who wants a marriage where each of the two partners always has a silly smile plastered on one's face?

There is an epilogue to this chapter—it involves some therapy I had in my life before I married him. I was taught that all issues had to be aired and cleaned up in order to have good relationships. This was drummed into me. When we married and began having little fights, I learned that he held the opposite belief—he was firm on the fact that painful feelings should be suppressed because if they were expressed they were too painful. I couldn't shake him from that belief, although I tried to, for years. I still think I'm in the right about this, but I gave up the battle because I wanted to win the war. Now I have learned how to back off when he gets like that. The therapists are not in the room with us.

His style and preference is that the less said after the argument is over, the better. I have learned that being married to a man who doesn't talk as much as I do means that the few humbly expressed words that are spoken by him are like gold nuggets. I should put them in the bank.

Chapter 32
PHOTOTOUR HOPPING AND PHOTOSHOPPING

We kept getting older, despite all the new curative medicines on the market. The country homestead had been sold and our hunting trips had given way to my husband's new obsessive and time-consuming hobby—fine art photography. Why not? I had always thought that pictures should stop being clichés. Who really wants to look at boring photos of what we did last summer? What is the point of accumulating endless prints of smiling faces stuck into albums which become, in turn, stuck into bookcases which become overcrowded and then have to be gone through? We can't even remember the names of the smiling faced people anyway.

I go along because I always do. Tomorrow we're driving to a real live rodeo to take photographs of guys and gals falling off horses. He had the idea that good photos taken at a rodeo where the action happened in split seconds was challenging and different. My idea of a photo at such a place that wouldn't be a cliché differed from his idea. I would have given a serious amount of money to have my picture taken on a bucking bronco and then sending that to my children with the notation: "Hi, kids, my Last Will is in the safe—don't make plans to come down this year." Naturally, I wouldn't have gotten on the animal—I would have selected the image that HE got and had him "Photoshop" my face onto some lady daredevil's body.

I had my own reasons for going with him and taking the camera. I liked going places that were NOT the same places I had always been going to. A new place could be in Yeehaw Junction,

Florida, or it could be in Bhutan. I didn't care. Taking photos was a lot of fun, and I always wanted the challenge of an off-the-wall destination. Big deal if I also learned how to take fairly good photographs—I wasn't going for the Pulitzer Prize. I was going for the raw amusement and competition of it. If he wanted to do it with a larger purpose, then he might need company. At first I believed that I either had to justify the costs of my transportation and lodging by carrying his photographic equipment or I had to be a somewhat serious shutterbug. My best-laid plans rested on incorrect assumptions, however. I had to do both.

So now we're at this rodeo building and he's paid the entries and we're unloading the stuff from his trunk. He's got this camera bag the size of a stadium which he hoists on his back and I'm fully aware he knows every last thing stuffed into it and precisely how to retrieve each individual item. I sort of know what's in my bag and how to retrieve each thing clumsily. Golfers have caddies and surfer hunks have bikini-clad babes and he had me and my slightly better than average expertise. I wanted to stay on Team Go Everywhere and Shoot Everything, so we picked out a fairly large camera bag for me and he taught me how to equip it and then strap it on myself and shlep it from the car to the point of interest. That means I'm going to be doing a dance like there's a gorilla hanging onto me while I look for a place to land my tuchus and also avoid falling onto an already seated rodeo patron. I can do it fairly well by now, although I have to be certain my cell phone is turned on so I can contact him—he is so far ahead of me he will have vanished into the crowd.

We had a pretty good rodeo shoot, but most of my pictures wound up capturing only about a third of each tumbled hotshot rider. My very best fine art shot was of a darling little girl in the stands with her face all smeared with chocolate ice cream. My worst example was a close-up of the crotch of an overweight pig handler who nearly landed on the empty seat next to me. His momentum had carried him a little too far. The shot was my worst because I got my finger in front of the lens. It blurred the most interesting feature.

The long trips and short excursions were welcomed by me, but they usually happened when I finally had secured some lucrative work, requiring me to juggle schedules and create acceptable excuses. I always had to keep my eye on what my dear husband was planning for the future because his plans dictated my plans—not vice versa.

"I'm officially retired now," he announced one day, sending jitters through my psyche. I would have preferred it if he had put it differently, like, "Honey, if I decide that my working for pay days are over, how will you feel?" But that wasn't his style. He must have figured that whatever he did, I'd pick up his decisions by osmosis and rearrange my life accordingly.

We had two homes during a five-year span, neither one of which had me believing that I was the lady of the house. Instead, I was the defender of my designated territory. We fought over the dining room furniture to be purchased for the Florida house dining area. He wanted a style that was manly and practical, while I wanted a style that would offer greater seating space and more storage. I won that debate, but that victory took a lot out of me. He was able to use leverage for multiple future purchases based on the fact he had given in about the dining room set. To this day, we have used our large dining room table about five times for "company." I failed to realize that not everybody in my crowd of friends and family in Illinois seemed poised and ready to hop on a plane and zoom over to South Florida.

I often stared at that dining room table and concentrated on what use we might make of it other than as a surface on which to put trial photographs, junk mail and old newspaper clippings. There had to be a sensible solution. I made resolutions to acquire local friends in our new neighborhood and invite them for dinner, but then I gave some consideration to the realities. I would have to haul out my dinnerware from my first marriage, reread my ancient cookbook to resuscitate recipes that were probably hopelessly outdated with ingredients no longer sold, and then blocked out some time to clean the entire house, including the closets. Mother's embedded messages did not die with her—they remained in my retained ten commandments of dos and don'ts, probably handed down to her from a prior generation of balabustes. The first commandment was: when company comes over for dinner, first clean out the closets—they might peek. The second commandment was: don't leave any telltale remnant of private bedroom activity. Put on fresh sheets and blankets even if nobody will ever see them. You don't need to know the other eight commandments, but they had little to do with the dinner to be served, other than the mandate that nobody should get even close to leaving the table hungry. I took my sweet time at inviting new friends over for dinner.

Mother always drilled into me that I would need a personal maid, but her reasons were not my reasons: She thought I was disorganized, so would need assistance. I thought I was too organized, so I might need assistance in order to maintain said organized existence. My predictions never quite transpired as predicted. I can count the times I used the service of a maid or cleaning helper on the fingers of one hand, so long as I don't use all the fingers.

He doesn't think the dining room table is a good use of space and I often see him eyeing it suspiciously. I know that one day when I return from one of my solo periodic trips to Chicago that I am going to come home and find the dining room set missing with portrait lighting equipment in its place. The humiliating part of this realization is that we will continue to have the same pattern of company for dinner despite the change in decor. I will suffer this change along with my gratefulness that I will be given another chance at exotic travel.

"What would you rather have?" he asks, with the sort of tone that predicts my precise answer, "Lots of furniture and cleaning help, or a trip to another part of the World where you can check out the beauty and diversity of the planet?"

"Can't I have a bit of coordinated furniture and maybe you have one or two fewer cameras or computers?"

"You don't really mean that."

"I know, but it came out of my mouth because of my background and the way I was raised."

"You were raised to be a housewife. You can remain a housewife, because I don't need your help to go on the trip I'm planning for next September."

"What trip now? Forget my domestic ways! You're not going anywhere out of this zip code without me!"

"The itinerary is on my desk. You can read it when you're finished reading Architectural Digest."

"I'll throw that issue away. I don't care where the trip is—I'm boning up on my photographic skills, like right away!"

"Big talk. Little action. You haven't even backed up your photos from our last drive to the Grand Canyon yet."

"I said I was getting around to it."

"Like you said you were going to read the instructions for your new SLR camera—the one I paid for with the expensive lens?"

"I read the important pages."

"Yes, the pages that contained the Table of Contents and the Glossary. How about the pages that explained how to use the menu? Or the ISO? All you do is ask me how to use the settings."

"Well, you're so deliciously convenient—you spend time learning the technology, while I just keep working and earning a paycheck."

"Just read the instructions and I'll add your name to the list of participants on this next tour."

"Yes, dear." I always went along after getting an earful of these exceptional arguments which brooked little resistance from me. I was lost before I even decided which little playing piece to put on the board. The only game I ever won with him was Scrabble, so he had stored the Scrabble set somewhere high in one of the closets where I would never find it again. But the good news took over my head—we were going to Peru. For an actual in-person visit to the ruins of Machu Pichu, I would do just about anything. I hurriedly reviewed my myriad files of photos from the Grand Canyon. They were pretty disgustingly amateurish, but that camera was now history. I made a new vow to become technologically superior—not to him, of course—just to a few little old ladies I knew.

That evening I reviewed the instructions for my new camera. I felt like a heroine with a mission—to try to figure out how to avoid blurring the subject's entire face and also take it out of the shadows. Heaven help me, I had to actually read beyond the Table of Contents.

Chapter 33
X NUMBER OF YEARS AND COUNTING

I read in the so-called "fluff" section of the so-called newspaper this morning about a couple that had been married 65 years and were still going strong. That made me really think: Were they lying when they said they still loved each other, and was the expression "still very much in love with her" as a direct quote from the old guy's mouth a throwaway line or the real McCoy? Since they were a Jewish couple, I should use the term "the real emes." I actually believed what I read—I think it's perfectly possible for a man to still love the same woman who put up with him all those years. But what about the woman? Did she know the difference between true love, adoration and commitment, as a totality of her loyal feelings, and that other tie that binds—duty, pity and blind attachment? I decided it didn't matter—they still went to bed together every night and got up with each other every morning. Their "embraceable you" picture was in the paper, most likely unphotoshopped.

I thought about my life and my marriage to my third husband. I could actually take a picture like that with him. I think he would take a picture like that with me if he had nothing better to do that snappable moment. How does a once-bitten twice mistaken lady of now really know where her mate stands in his inner convictions? If he continues to eye me suspiciously whenever I leave some of the dirty breakfast dishes on the table, do I have a cause for concern? If he says nothing injurious but walks around the house with an unspoken message that reads, "Don't even think of messing with me today!" should I begin reading Match.com or checking the laundry for lip gloss stains? They say that it's the little things that count. Make that infraction about the dishes I mentioned above even smaller: pretend I left one slightly stained coffee cup where I shouldn't have and abandoned the kitchen area for my own pursuits—would he inwardly growl and think rude thoughts that might make him shut down when I wanted him to help me clean out something that I messed up without his help? In other words, am I a keeper wife?

When I married him I knew I was a fixer-upper. When he married me he knew he was taking the biggest gamble of his life because he said so. His relatives said so. Even his horoscope wasn't particularly favorable that year. He didn't believe in horoscope stuff, but somebody he knew did. So what went right? I returned my thoughts to the article in today's newspaper. That couple married in 1945. I was eight years old in 1945. That was the year my brother was born. My most vivid memory of the day of his birth was my really nasty temper tantrum in the waiting room of the hospital because I wasn't allowed in the birth area due to my tender years. I'm sure I scuffed my orthopedic shoes kicking the floor till the shine wore off. I can't forget that day because for the first time in my life, my carefully honed cajoling and manipulating techniques weren't working.

I figured that if my mother could have gotten out of bed and done something about it, she would have made sure that I got a new toy, some cookies and a promise of more when she brought the new bundle home. But she was doped up and my father was busy handing out cigars with blue wrappers. A natural born son was the requirement for a man of his background—European immigrant of the struggling class—not too far removed from pograms or ghettoization. I could tell that he was happy as a puppet on the strings of the elders—father of the next line of descendants to carry his proud name. My eight-year-old wisdom had recorded enough rampant sexism to know that I had just been outclassed—

relegated to the category of that other variety of human. I do remember wanting to make fast friends with this newcomer in the
nursery because he would soon be in charge.

But things changed a lot in the last 65 years. I'm the survivor
of those other three. My brother has been dead since 1978, my
father since 1962 and my mother since 1993. Many of the rules
they promulgated got mixed up with the new learning, the wrong
learning, the disregarded pure learning and the unlearning. I
get my code of conduct from my fear of failure and my need to
be playfully engaged. Where is my moral compass? Is it similar
to that same compass that my new husband strapped on my wrist
more than once so that I wouldn't get lost in the woods? The one
I couldn't quite read? Am I still kicking my shoes on some floor
somewhere because I can't get I want? Is everything in this book
the new scuff mark?

I think that's enough philosophy. I'm going to quit shortly.
But before I do, I have to take another run through that column
about that couple's 65th wedding anniversary.

Let me see here—it says that the fellow had been in a con-
centration camp and was freed at the end of 1944, 19 years old,
skinny and hairless. He was introduced to this beautiful seventeen-
year-old girl and he insisted on talking to her for longer than just
a few minutes. They lived in cruel regimes in Europe and somehow got to America—the land of freedom. Like many immigrants,
they worked hard and prospered. Their lives went uphill and then
settled in on a plateau of fulfillment, or so the sweetly written column reports. It doesn't say that they never argued or acted com-
petitively, so I assume that one or both of them got angry at least
some of the time. I have to believe in the imperfection of a perfect
marriage, or I will see that I am living a sham life.

Does it make a difference that my father came to the shores
of this country in 1917 from a background that he never would

260

discuss? He was never in prison and he never cheated anybody. My mother survived him by thirty years and in that whole time had one date with a fellow that she described as "nice, but not my type." Her expectations were different from my expectations. My expectations have changed over the years. The following list describes my vocational ambitions to the best of my recollection, in the order of when I dreamed them up:

Movie star, as in Shirley Temple

Comedienne, as in Fannie Bryce

Sportscaster, as in Bert Wilson

Astronomer, as in the fellow who took the photographs that hung on the walls at the Adler Planetarium

Writer, as in Lewis Carroll

Poet, as in Robert Louis Stevenson

Journalist, as in the lead character in the old soap opera, "Front Page Farrell"

Wife, as in my mother's best friend who was married to the furrier

President, as in Harry S. Truman who said that the buck stopped there

Cateress, balabuste and hotel manager, as in Jennie Grossinger

Gay divorcee, as in Ginger Rogers

Tax lawyer, as in how I actually ended up

261

Adviser to the confused couples of today, as in me as the woman who continuously advises; and

Designated quip provider of the workplace, as in any woman who can make a few people laugh and forget the mess they think they're in;

I decided to end the above list with a semi-colon because a semi-colon means you're not quite finished.

I asked my husband what career objectives he has harbored in his entire life. He gave me the following list:

Teacher/Economist
Cartoonist

That's it—that's his list. He had to choose his calling when he graduated with a Masters Degree in Economics. He took his port-folio of drawings of funny men with big noses to the animation studios in Manhattan and got a job. When he retired he wanted to do something else which did not include going to any office anywhere. So now he takes really good photographs. One day he may take a prize-winner of me, but that hasn't happened yet. That doesn't mean I'm not a prize—it only means that he hasn't yet come up with the vision that takes the shot of me at my most mem-orable against a background that fits the mood that some contest judge submits to some publication that wins some prize that some people think didn't deserve to win. Got that straight? There is no absolute win.

And readers of these words, I conclude with the following: If there is no absolute win, then it would appear that there should be no need for domestic wars or fierce competition between soul-mates. But here's the dilemma: If you remove all or most of the fury of the competitive battles, then don't you end up with frustrat-ed partners in a relationship? You might also be closing off part of the fun of growing old together. Think about that for awhile, and, while you're pondering and cogitating about whether you prefer a placid sea over five-foot waves, rest assured that I'll be around, brassy and rebellious as ever. And oh yes, if you wonder what I'm up to, there's a pretty good chance I'll be somewhere in my kitchen, scrubbing our place mats to perfection.

Love, from me.

THE END

Endnotes

1   1959 movie directed by Mel Ferrer, starring Audrey Hepburn and Anthony Perkins

2   1947 movie directed by Chester Erskine

3   Book by Daphne du Maurier, made into an Alfred Hitchcock film

4   Years later I learned that Annie's rough sketches had been made into a four panel artwork painted in acrylics and that it hangs today at the Palos Heights Public Library in suburban Cook County.

5   nuttiness

6   Yiddish expression for industrious woman with strong domestic skills

7   he did the chain sawing—I did the cringing

8   Yiddish word for 'troubles', only more so

9   The swear words are just too evil to print in this innocent volume

8931487R0

Made in the USA
Charleston, SC
27 July 2011